The Wormwood File

The Wormwood File

E-mail from Hell

Jim Forest

ORBIS BOOKS

Maryknoll, New York 10545

Founded in 1970, Orbis Books endeavors to publish works that enlighten the mind, nourish the spirit, and challenge the conscience. The publishing arm of the Maryknoll Fathers and Brothers, Orbis seeks to explore the global dimensions of the Christian faith and mission, to invite dialogue with diverse cultures and religious traditions, and to serve the cause of reconciliation and peace. The books published reflect the views of their authors and do not represent the official position of the Maryknoll Society. To learn more about Maryknoll and Orbis Books, please visit our website at www.maryknoll.org.

Library of Congress Cataloging-in-Publication Data

Forest, James H.
  The Wormwood file : e-mail from hell / Jim Forest.
    p. cm.
  ISBN 1-57075-554-X (pbk.)
  1. Christianity. I. Title.
  BR125.F617 2004
  230—dc22
                        2004007148

For Daniel

"We may not pay Satan reverence, for that would be indiscreet, but we can at least respect his talents. A person who has for untold centuries maintained the imposing position of spiritual head of four-fifths of the human race, and political head of the whole of it, must be granted the possession of executive abilities of the loftiest order."

—Mark Twain

"There are two equal and opposite errors into which our race can fall about the devils. One is to disbelieve in their existence. The other is to believe, and to feel an excessive and unhealthy interest in them."

—C. S. Lewis, preface to *The Screwtape Letters*

Foreword

Demon-to-demon correspondence is not the kind of writing we often gain access to or even imagine exists. Aren't devils a figment of our superstitious ancestors' fevered imaginations? A pre-scientific way of explaining madness, illness, wars, plagues, famines, and other misfortunes? A way of blaming invisible beings for all those actions once regarded as sins but now seen, in the clear light of scientific day, as mistakes or misunderstandings?

It's not a bad age to be a demon. They have a freer hand so long as we regard them as nonexistent. How can what doesn't exist do us any harm?

Would that they were the nothings we imagine. Unfortunately, not only do they exist, but they are damnably clever. They even write letters.

How did I obtain an exchange of hellish e-mail? It was thanks to a chance meeting at a venerable but unpretentious pub in Oxford, the Eagle & Child, where anything that interferes with quiet conversation is unwelcome. Though most of the pub's clients are known only to their friends and families, many luminaries have lifted a pint at this establishment, including J. R. R. Tolkien and C. S. Lewis, yet there isn't a clipping on the walls suggesting that such words as "hobbit" and "Aslan" were heard there before they were heard anywhere else.

This past May, while in that academic town for a conference and having ordered an ale at the Eagle & Child, I discovered that the man standing next to me at the bar was an "I.T."

specialist. "Eye Tea?" I asked. "Information technology," he replied, recognizing me as a throwback to the Gutenberg era.

Forgiving my ignorance, he went on to explain he was in the midst of a project being conducted at Magdalen College. His task was to find more effective ways to defend the university's computers from viruses, worms and other unwelcome "e-guests."

I said it sounded like tedious work.

"Sometimes it is," he told me, "but there are occasional discoveries that make it more than worthwhile. Just yesterday I managed to hack my way through the firewalls of Hell."

I chuckled. Clearly he was joking.

"I know it sounds altogether unlikely," he responded, "but I'm not kidding. Using the Google search engine, I meant to type in the name of a fellow researcher whose web site I wanted to visit—a man named Wornwood. By a slip of the index finger I found a link to a web site for the domain 'Wormwood'! It was a very austere page, simply the word 'Wormwood' in red gothic letters on a dark grey background —a page with a seriously diabolic look! But the site was password protected. I couldn't stroll right in."

He paused for a long sip of ale.

"You must understand that I'm the sort of person who finds locked doors a challenge," he said. "At least on the web, I'm pretty good at breaking and entering. But I might never have managed to find a way in, or even have had the motivation, had I not been a C. S. Lewis fan. You must have heard of him, but have you ever read *The Screwtape Letters*? Very worthwhile. It's a collection of letters from a senior demon named Screwtape to a dense apprentice named Wormwood published sixty years ago during the last world war. Anyway, after several bad guesses, I typed 'Screwtape' into the password field on the theory that sometimes the simplest key is the one that works—and bingo, the door opened! As I was soon to discover, I was in that part of the web that is farthest below sea level."

I asked what he had found.

"Sadly, not a lot. Within minutes whoever guards the site was on to me. I lost my connection and my computer crashed. When I was up and running again, there was no longer a Wormwood site. It had vanished. But during my short visit, I had managed to download a file of e-mail sent by Wormwood to an up-and-coming junior devil named Greasebeek. Unfortunately Greasebeek's half of the exchange wasn't part of the file, though it's easy enough to guess his side of it. If you care to see the archive, I can pass it on to you. Just give me your e-mail address. You do have one?"

Luckily I did. The file was waiting for me when I checked my e-mail that night.

I read it immediately, then responded with the suggestion it should be published. My new-found friend—let me call him Albion—said this was out of the question: "Believe me, my job prospects would not be enhanced by having my name on the cover of a collection of e-mail from Hell. The prudent scholar who wants to keep his academic career on the right track would do well not to confess his suspicion that there are demons about." He suggested I take charge of the file. And so I have.

Several friends I've shared the file with have doubted the authenticity of the exchange. One colleague regards it as ridiculous to think non-physical beings, should they exist, would have any need for e-mail. (It's my view that e-mail, being so radically a non-physical medium, is ideal for demons.)

One friend asked if I had done a "background check" on Albion. The answer is no.

I freely admit there is no way to prove these messages are what they claim to be, only that the man who passed them on to me has good taste in pubs and ale. He doesn't impress me as suffering a compulsion to conduct séances or sell snake oil to the gullible. One of the striking things about him is that he has no interest in selling anything.

In a recent note he points out that, even for a hardened atheist, belief in Hell doesn't require a leap of faith: "Any sensible person should find Hell a good deal easier to believe in than Heaven. All you need to do is think of how many ways we've come up with to harm each other, a list that gets constantly longer as we migrate from war to war. For most of us, glimpses of Heaven are not as easily come by." These are not the thoughts of a man who has the Mad Hatter in his family tree.

No doubt there are those readers who will be tempted to think I'm the one who descends from the Mad Hatter. I console myself by recalling that Lewis must have endured similar suspicions when he published his collection more than half a century ago.

Jim Forest
Third Sunday of Lent: The Veneration of the Cross
March 14, 2004

Inbox

	From	Subject	Page
1.	Wormwood	Teamwork	3
2.	Wormwood	The real world	7
3.	Wormwood	Noise	11
4.	Wormwood	True religion	14
5.	Wormwood	The spiritual path	17
6.	Wormwood	Coping with the Enemy's texts	21
7.	Wormwood	Loving yourself	24
8.	Wormwood	Choice	28
9.	Wormwood	Play plus boy	32
10.	Wormwood	Temptation and guilt	35
11.	Wormwood	Hurting no one	40
12.	Wormwood	E-rage	43
13.	Wormwood	Prayer in the trenches	47
14.	Wormwood	Free-range fish	52
15.	Wormwood	Rush hour	55

16.	Wormwood	Perfectionism	59
17.	Wormwood	Theological argument	63
18.	Wormwood	Which brand?	68
19.	Wormwood	Zero moments	72
20.	Wormwood	Postcards from home	77
21.	Wormwood	War	80
22.	Wormwood	Holy writ	86
23.	Wormwood	Anticipate the quarry's next move	89
24.	Wormwood	Self-esteem	92
25.	Wormwood	Icons	96
26.	Wormwood	Victimhood	99
27.	Wormwood	Rights	104
28.	Wormwood	Saints	107
29.	Wormwood	Damnation	111
30.	Wormwood	A close call	113

Wormwood Message 1

TO: Greasebeek

FROM: Wormwood

SUBJECT: Teamwork

My dearest, most congenial Greasebeek,

Of course I am at your service. "Teamwork" is a popular word among humans these days. We could use more of it in Hell. I also recall that I was once as clueless as you are.

Yes, you have had a setback. That's obvious. But don't be so quick to hit the alarm button! A cool head is always a good thing, no matter how hot the furnace. I agree that your client's situation is threatening, but only mildly so. There is no reason to regard him as a lost cause or yourself in a room with no exits.

So he has bought a CD of monks chanting. I can assure you that most people who buy recordings of Gregorian chant, Orthodox liturgies, Black spirituals, and the like rarely become Christians. I know you will find this hard to imagine, but they barely listen to what is being sung. The words, even if in a language they happen to understand, are merely restful, pleasant sounds. These recordings are supposed to reduce stress—that is their main selling point. They are non-prescription tranquilizers. In any event, your client will find music of this type far more easily in music shops than in actual churches. There isn't one church in a thousand that has music that compares favorably with what people buy in music shops. I've known people to give up on Christianity simply because the music in actual churches doesn't measure up to recordings!

We had a case recently of a man leaving a certain parish because he didn't like the sound system. He has yet to find a parish that measures up to his artistic standards. I doubt he ever will.

If you wore shoes, you would wear them out looking for a parish that provides music any record company would want to record.

You say your client is listening to these recordings on a daily basis while driving to work and occasionally at home. The thing to guard against is his connecting the music with actual Christian belief. If he thinks of it at all, help him to regard the Christian music he enjoys as primitive "folk art." This is what you need to encourage.

Don't misunderstand me. I'm not suggesting that you should be complacent about the sort of music he is playing. Clearly the content is dangerous and even the music itself, as pure sound, suggests what the Enemy refers to as "the kingdom of Heaven." Beauty is always a danger. It does happen from time to time that even one phrase from a song or hymn will set in motion ideas that can undermine many years of hard work on our part.

If the "folk art" line of defense fails, at vulnerable moments plant the thought that the people who sing such music are doing it purely for the sake of art—or, better yet, for money—and don't believe what they're singing any more than a politician believes his own speeches.

You mention that he has learned by heart a few stanzas of "Amazing Grace." If you hear him humming that appalling tune, the danger will pass if you can make him recall some particularly ugly item in the news or hideous episode in human history. What good is "amazing grace" if terrorists are blowing up children or if people are starving to death or if plagues are killing thousands? Stick with the slogan that "no good God would permit evil things to happen" and you will have nothing to worry about.

The man who wrote "Amazing Grace" was nearly ours, by the way—a slave trader much of his life. A sad tale, that one. His guardian demon, who failed to see what was going on right under his nose, is still paying the price for letting him fall into the Enemy's hands. (Never forget for a moment that, just as there are rewards for achievement, there are penalties for failure. There is more to Hell than you yet know.)

Happily, your client seems so put off by "organized religion" that there is probably no need to wave headlines or history books at him.

"Organized religion"—what a useful phrase that's been! Isn't it amazing how many people appreciate organized health care, organized education, organized garbage collection, organized mail delivery, organized beer breweries, and organized film making, and yet without batting an eye embrace the idea that everyone would be better off without organized religion? Don't you love it? The widespread acceptance of this term, pronounced as if it were a disease, has been one of our greatest triumphs, making your work a hundred times easier than it was in former times, and all the more so in simple, low-level cases like the one you have.

Did you know that my mentor and uncle, the renowned Screwtape, was one of those who did the most to make this phrase so popular? He is an example to us all, though one has always to take care not to offend or disappoint one of his magnitude! You may have heard rumors of my near catastrophe at his hands not many decades ago when I was much less experienced in the management of souls. Luckily I happened to have discovered a few details about a failure of his that he was desperately eager should never be reported. This item of intelligence reversed my fortunes and even put me up a notch.

Warmly yours,

Wormwood

Wormwood Message 2

TO: Greasebeek

FROM: Wormwood

SUBJECT: The real world

My dearest Greasebeek,

In your previous e-mail message you were nervous about a shift in your client's musical tastes, but can you imagine what might happen if he were to disconnect himself, even partially, from his TV? What good is a guardian devil who notices dust but overlooks boulders?

You consigned to a mere PS the decision made by your client and his wife—by the way, what do you know about her?—to shift their television from the living room to the spare room in order "to get it out of the center of their lives." Especially disturbing is his remark about needing to take steps "to build up a spiritual life."

At least they haven't completely gotten rid of the TV. Even so, this has the potential of moving many things in the wrong direction.

Your old instructor Grimshaw assured me you were clever, but I begin to have my doubts. How could you fail to see this danger approaching and neglect to take appropriate preventative measures?

You might at least have suggested placing it in the bedroom, which in many cases is a better location for a television than the living room. It is not unusual for bedroom sets to run all night, with those who doze in the electronic glare waking up fitfully to catch disturbing fragments of whatever happens to be on as the night progresses—scenes of murder and mayhem, or often violent, semi-pornographic films. In fact these days there might be nothing "semi" about it.

Even in the case of those who at last turn it off, the presence of bedroom television will usually mean less reading, less talking and less quiet unwinding before falling asleep—thus a more tired, more irritable person the next day. Most important, an active television, even when it is running only as background noise, means less prayer, or none.

But perhaps your man is another type and may succeed in reducing the time he spends paralyzed in front of a television. You mention several programs your client used to watch regularly, programs generally regarded as "wholesome," "inspiring," etc., suggesting it might actually be in our interest that he intends to see less TV. You seem to think it's a triumph that he might miss the occasional documentary about pilgrims making their way to some pathetic shrine or nuns serving the poor or something else equally distasteful. But all these things are entirely harmless so long as they are just images on a television screen. The viewer will feel virtuous simply because he is watching charitable ladies doing good deeds in distant places that he will never visit and among the sorts of people he carefully avoids in real life. The main fact is that, watching these holy nuns, your man is safe in a dream world, doing nothing, not lifting a finger for anyone, not even saying a prayer or parting with his loose change. It hardly matters what he fantasizes about from time to time so long as it's only star-gazing—or saint-gazing. (Yes, of course, demon-gazing pleases us far better. You must do what you can to speed the day.)

What *is* dangerous is your client taking charge of his eyes. I don't think you yet grasp that if we can turn a man's eyes in the right direction, he's ours right down to his toenails. Own a man's eyes and you own the man.

I had a client once who attended church services for more than a year, even sang in the choir for several months. I was beginning to think she was a lost cause. Luckily for us, however, she never broke the habit of watching television whenever she was alone. There was always something to remind her that "the real world" has nothing to do "with some alleged all-powerful deity," as she used to say, once she had seen the darkness. Finally she decided that going to church was as childish as believing in Tinker Bell. The lady died a few years ago and is today safely below.

Take heart. You have lost a battle but certainly not the war. At the very least, you can count on your client's friends to be raising their eyebrows at this repositioning of the TV. If you play your cards right, he'll soon be worrying that he is being seen by his friends as slightly cracked if not a total nut case. Keep in mind that peer group disapproval, even when only imagined, is no small thing. The average

human being would rather be regarded as a criminal than
a crackpot.

Yours warmly,

Wormwood

PS Kindly avoid the e-mail shorthand! After a little research,
I've learned that LOL means lots of luck, but when writing
me, write in complete sentences. I am not a teenager and
this is not chatroom doodling.

Wormwood Message 3

TO: Greasebeek

FROM: Wormwood

SUBJECT: Noise

My dearest Greasebeek,

I notice that you are putting too much stress on what your client is *doing* rather than what he is *thinking*. Regard him as a ship. Your task is to take charge not of the rigging or the sails but of the rudder. His thoughts are the rudder.

The battleground is the human mind. Reshape what he thinks and the deeds you intend for him will follow. There are ideas with wider jaws and sharper teeth than any dragon.

Consider the television's current exile in the spare room, a minor matter and yet an area not to be overlooked. If you can promote the idea that he's been just slightly extreme in moving the TV to a new location and that "a little TV watching is harmless," it may not be long before the TV is back where it used to be or that there are even two in the house instead of one. Play your cards right and he may be staring at the tube more at the end of the year than he was at the beginning—and thus be in a more passive, compliant state.

Meanwhile, the danger is that he will use time that was once devoted to television for activities that threaten our goals. In the Enemy's book, the New Testament, there is a "parable" about a woman who managed to get rid of one demon that inhabited her house, only to have seven new ones come to take its place. The point is that vacuums are short-lived. If the space created by getting rid of something isn't filled by something of a different character, things even worse than what was briefly swept away will be drawn into the vacuum. Indeed!

Fortunately, what is more probable is that your client will panic when faced with silence and the difficulties of building up "a spiritual life." While he may occasionally claim he wishes he had more peace and quiet, in practice he is bound to find the reality of peace and quiet impossible to endure.

You must have heard in the Academy how, in the course of the last century or two, especially in countries that regard themselves as "developed," constant noise has become normal and even necessary. Pure silence has become hardly bearable for millions of people. Your client lives in an age of honking cars, shrieking ambulances and police cars, the noise of motorcycles, garbage trucks, televisions, radios, airplanes, helicopters, telephones, and shouting neighbors. The din he takes for granted would have driven his ancestors insane, but he lives happily in the midst of all that cacophony without even considering ear plugs.

While your client is currently trying to be an exception, look around and notice how many people these days have radios or televisions or Walkmans and the like going all day long—

in some cases even when they're sleeping. Noise dependency has become one of the most popular addictions, yet so "normal" it isn't even recognized as an addiction.

Yours warmly,

Wormwood

Wormwood Message 4

TO: Greasebeek

FROM: Wormwood

SUBJECT: True religion

My dearest Greasebeek,

So the television remains in the spare room even though you can see he hardly knows what to do in the living room without it, attempting to read but "finding it hard going." You mention that he's boasting to friends about "shaking the TV habit."

For the moment forget about getting the television back in the living room. There is another course of action that would meet our needs just as well, if not better. What you must suggest to your client is that he embrace the idea that television itself "is the very devil" and that the remote control he has been neglecting in recent days is nothing less than the key to the gates of Hell. He could become so obsessed with waging war on the TV that this could become the organizing principle of his life. Before you know it he will begin to divide the world up into those who agree with him and those who don't. Heaven defend those who don't!

There's nothing like a heady cause to drive wedges between people. People with dozens of good qualities suddenly are placed on the enemies list because of a disagreement over some detail of life. Properly nursed, an aversion to television can become your client's religion.

Perhaps you wonder, "Why would we want anyone to be religious?" Ah, but we do! Never forget that human beings are basically religious. It's a key element in their design. Did you never read in the Academy that famous passage from the Wretched Augustine about how their "hearts are restless until they rest in God" and so on and so forth? It's in the grain.

But religion need not be only some God-centered faith. It is anything they do to cope with that restlessness—anything that gives their life purpose, meaning, and direction. Our job is to make sure it's a religion that points them in the right direction—a direction other than what the Enemy has in mind. Take my word for it, almost anything will do.

There are people whose religion is sports. They know more about a certain team than they know about their children. The religion can be politics, money, the environment, war, peace, mental health, vitamins, sex, music, muscle growth, clothing, human rights, monarchy, anarchism, mountain climbing, movie stars, home decoration, music—any cause or obsession whatsoever. It doesn't matter what it is so long as it takes center stage in a person's life, filling what might be called the "God space."

Do your job well and you'll see that *any* hobby, ideology, or cause can be made into a whirlpool. If it's an ideological cause, you'll know you've achieved your goal when the person has become a ranter. There are more vegetarians than cannibals in Hell.

Yours warmly,

Wormwood

Wormwood Message 5

TO: Greasebeek

FROM: Wormwood

SUBJECT: The spiritual path

My dearest Greasebeek,

So he has taken to telling friends he is on a "a spiritual path." Why does this worry you so? After all, who could know better than a purely spiritual being like yourself that even humans need a spiritual life? But it must be the *right* sort of spiritual life, and here our views are diametrically opposed to those of our Enemy.

The fact that he went into a "New Age" shop can actually be seen in positive rather than negative terms. Certainly you have heard of, perhaps even met, His Grimitude, my dear uncle Screwtape, to whom I owe so much despite the unpleasant memory of his once having nearly eaten me alive after I let a client slip through my fingers. Not a pleasant memory, but the past is past and I rarely worry about his appetite getting the best of him so long as I take reasonable precautions.

It was my cherished uncle Screwtape who lately pointed out that the New Age movement is a religion best symbolized by the credit card. As he so astutely noted, "they might as well put a sign over the door saying 'Enlightenment for Sale.'" Those without credit cards are of little interest.

While there are more New Age movements than there are quills on a porcupine, invariably each and every one of them puts the stress on individual happiness. There is no Ash Wednesday or Good Friday, no cross, no repentance, no dying to self, no laying down your life for others, no self-giving love, no obligation to forgive, but rather self-esteem, self-affirmation, personal fulfillment, good health, success in life, and finally reincarnation with the assurance that one can always do better in the next life and eventually achieve perfect bliss. There are few if any burdensome rules and there is little or no interest in truth as such. Instead, you can have as many "truths" as you like. You are welcome to believe or not believe that God exists.

I recall one famous guru who liked to say, "Atheist? Believer? It's all the same, for words can never contain truth." No matter what the man said, it was always with a beaming smile. What a fortune was spent on that man's glittering teeth, his brilliant grin! His listeners found him absolutely charming and loved giving him money and gifts. They practically wallpapered their homes with his photos. Long before their beloved guru died, they had made him a millionaire many times over. I can assure you the man is no longer smiling.

Another plus is that, whatever their differences, these New Age groups are unanimous in giving Christianity harsh reviews. It's the one religion they dismiss out of hand, calling it the source of countless evils. Name anything wrong in the world today or yesterday and they will explain that it's chiefly because of Christianity. Believe me, there is no tribe in any jungle whose religion is condemned and rejected so absolutely. Comfort yourself with the thought that your client is not likely to find a cross or anything specifically Christian in any New Age shop. There will be books from nearly every religion but no Bibles. Satan be praised, Christianity is out of fashion—at least among the clever.

You mention that your client purchased a book about Buddha and Jesus at the New Age shop. Did I detect a note of anxiety? Rest assured there is nothing to worry about. While I haven't read the book in question, I can promise you that Jesus will be treated simply as one of numerous "great teachers" and will rank well below the Buddha. The authors of these books always present themselves as rescuing Jesus from the Church, and this serves our needs perfectly. Your client will not be harmed by a churchless Jesus: no tradition, no truth, no disciplines, no community, no creed, no gospel, no sacraments—just a collection of whatever sayings aren't at odds with New Age sensitivities, with a marked preference for Gnostic sources rather than the New Testament. What could be better? May your client read his new book for an hour each day and give copies to all his friends.

Your efforts have taken a turn for the better. At last you are making headway. Just don't rest on your laurels. Keep in mind that the Enemy is also represented at your client's side twenty-four hours a day. It's a great pity we can never quite make out what that other spirit—the "guardian angel"—is saying. But we can make shrewd guesses. Your counterpart will be searching for opportunities in all these setbacks: perhaps a whisper to your client that Jesus must have been something more than simply another great teacher for the world's calendar to be organized around his birth, or the suggestion that the main item in a New Age shop isn't the merchandise but the cash register.

Stay alert. The wind has shifted in your favor, but your achievement is still only superficial.

Yours warmly,

Wormwood

Wormwood Message 6

TO: Greasebeek

FROM: Wormwood

SUBJECT: Coping with the Enemy's texts

My dearest Greasebeek,

Finally you have provided news of your client's wife. It's essential that you and her guardian demon coordinate your activities. For the moment she is clearly a danger, but with only a little effort, she can become an ally—in which case we will land two birds with one arrow.

It is of course alarming that she has suggested a visit to church. You and your colleague must join forces to prevent that. I will return to this topic before concluding this message. But first some other matters.

You mention in your e-mail that she recently purchased a Bible. You say she left it on the coffee table in the living room where your client can't help but notice it. I wouldn't be too concerned about this. My guess is that it is less a religious event than a round of combat with her husband. What better means of putting herself on the moral high ground than to bring a Bible into the house? It is only a prop in a play.

You comment that so far she has done nothing more with it than randomly flip through the pages. I'm not surprised. This is in fact the fate of the vast majority of Bibles. People get them with the best of intentions, glance at them occasionally, and then after a few months forget about them. No matter how "modern" the translation, people find much of what they read bewildering or even offensive. For some reason, they think that the Bible should be as simple to read and easy to understand as a newspaper. In most cases it doesn't take long before they give up. If all the unread or neglected Bibles could be turned back into trees, you would hear no more talk among humans about endangered forests.

Finally, there is the matter of the wife's suggestion that they "see what services at the local church are like." This remark may be as insignificant as the Bible now decorating the living room—or it may be that the Enemy is gaining ground and using her to undermine your recent achievements with your client. It may even be connected to her growing interest in maternity. Believe me, considerations of motherhood tend to open all sorts of dangerous channels of thought.

Your client's aversion to "organized religion" may well prove defense enough. Let him remind his wife of how bored she was on those occasions when she was made to go to church as a child, how dull the sermons were, how confined and uncomfortable she felt in the pews, how many times she was told to be quiet, how often she asked, "Will it be over soon?"

Should that fail, let him remind her of how irritating their church-going next-door neighbors are with their blaring music and piggish way of parking. Do you really want to spend your free time with people like that?

Finally, make sure that he notices and passes on to her any news reports on the sins of the clergy. We've had quite a good run with clerical scandals lately. What we want people to see is often on page one: the seduction of choir boys, extramarital affairs, clerical involvement in pornographic web sites, and on and on. While in reality all this involves only a tiny fragment of the clergy, often individuals who long ago left or were dismissed from ministry, there are many people who now regard every priest or minister with instant suspicion. This should make your job much easier than mine was when I was at your level, you lucky devil.

Yours warmly,

Wormwood

Wormwood Message 7

TO: Greasebeek
FROM: Wormwood
SUBJECT: Loving yourself

My dearest Greasebeek,

You are too worried about their marriage—the occasional
love-making, meals out, chocolates on Valentine's Day, etc.
Such gestures and flashes of contact are common in many
marriages that are inching their way down a dead-end street.

You said they have been married several years? Then you can
assume the romance is over and long-distance love has not
yet taken root. Look at the objective situation. Both husband
and wife have demanding jobs which neither especially
enjoys but in which each feels success is a must, partly for
financial reasons but still more because every social tide has
carried them in this direction. The result is the happy fact
that by the time they get home both of them are tired and
irritable. It requires only minor influence on your part to see
that your client's irritations are taken out on his wife.

Marriage is not nearly as secure an arrangement as it used to
be. These days one-third of all marriages end in divorce, and
the percentage keeps rising. Many marriages are a battlefield.

Thanks to the efforts of your predecessors, it is a dogma of contemporary culture that the number-one task in life is to love yourself, period. Every man and woman knows this. In practice this means asserting yourself, being on the lookout for yourself, and under all conditions leading your own life. The language of love has become the language of narcissism.

What happens in many marriages resembles what goes on in business negotiations—a constant nervous measuring and balancing of what each party does or fails to do: how many dishes washed, how many meals cooked, how much cleaning done, how much laundry washed, how much money spent by whom. From the first moment of their relationship, partners anticipate the last moment.

Yet, in this particular marriage, not everything is as we might wish. You mention the wife recently referring to "the ticking of her biological clock," then yesterday stopping on the street to look into a baby carriage and remarking to your client later in the day how "amazed" she was at the infant's gaze and sudden smile. Then there was the article about natural childbirth she left on the coffee table. Pay attention to what is happening! While she hasn't said anything aloud yet and very likely hardly dares think it to herself, she is beginning to think that having a child might not be such a bad thing and in small ways is making a vague longing visible to her husband.

Recall what you were taught in training at the Academy: almost all humans eventually want children, even when they have spent years carefully avoiding having any. I once had a client who left a Catholic seminary just weeks before he was to be ordained. The man explained to his bewildered rector that he was leaving because of his children. "What children?" the rector asked, suddenly imagining scandalous things about the seminarian's private life. The man answered, "The children I have not yet had." This was far from my finest hour. I had been too complacent about his ambition to become a priest. It was my expectation that he would get around to sex, but *after* ordination. In what is supposed to be a celibate environment, that would have been most entertaining. Instead, he got married, had four children, and now is a grandfather. I regret to say that through all those years he has remained a conscientious church-goer well known for his generosity, very rarely giving us a toehold. I had an unpleasant memo about the case from my department head only yesterday.

Luckily your client, far from wanting children, is still more boy than man. He's frightened to death of parenthood. But take care. Such attitudes can change in the blink of an eye.

This shift in the wife's thinking clearly has been felt by your client or he wouldn't be making those anxious comments to her about how unlucky the neighbors are "to be saddled with kids," remarking how expensive children are, and being so careful about birth control. While neither admits it out loud, if you listen closely you will discover between the lines of their conversations that not a day passes without veiled debate about the possibility of parenthood.

Regarding your client's wife, no doubt your colleague will concentrate on her fears: "Am I ready to be a mother? What will this mean for my career? Isn't the world too overcrowded and dangerous? How can we be sure it will be a healthy child? Am I not a little too old?"

The danger with children is no doubt obvious to you, even if you have forgotten what you learned at the Academy. Almost invariably a child pulls the borders of the parents' souls outward. Parenthood dramatically changes the contours of a life, and rarely for the better. Even before actual birth, when the child is no more than a slight swelling of its mother's belly, you would notice a radical change in your client's priorities— much less absorption in himself, much more astonishment. A man who had long since been stripped of any sense of awe about existence, human and otherwise, would suddenly be chattering to all and sundry about "the miracle of life."

A word to the wise: If you detect your client wavering in his objections to becoming a parent, avoid a frontal attack and instead promote the idea that children are, of course, a good thing and probably should come eventually, *but not yet.* Remind your client, whenever he gets starry-eyed about children or simply wants to please his wife, that having a baby would inevitably require a larger place to live, more money, more security in his job, all sorts of costly and complicated arrangements for child care, and—not least—a huge reduction of their freedom.

You might also let him ponder the fact that, when there is a baby in his wife's arms, he will no longer be at stage center. Let him fear the loss of love. Let him fear a child not yet conceived. Let him fear that he will be a terrible father.

Keep in mind that there is no such thing as too much fear— except fear of our Enemy above. *That* fear is a fear you must never encourage.

Yours warmly,

Wormwood

Wormwood Message 8

TO: Greasebeek

FROM: Wormwood

SUBJECT: Choice

My dearest Greasebeek,

No wonder you let a month go by without a word. Your client's wife is pregnant? You told me she was only glancing into baby carriages. How could you have been so unaware of the direction in which things were moving? Have you been reading comic books? Playing solitaire? Watching MTV?

Luckily, it is an "unplanned" pregnancy. What an interesting term! Times have changed. Unplanned pregnancies used to be the only kind. Fortunately, your client's wife was only just beginning to want a baby. Now that she finds herself eight months from having an actual infant in her arms, we can assume she feels torn between happiness and panic, with panic often having the upper hand. Meanwhile—lucky you—a baby is not at all on your client's wish list.

In other words, we are talking about a reversible situation. All your client needs to do is talk his wife into having an abortion, which she has doubtless been considering anyway. With a little effort on your part, your client will find himself

convinced that the future of the marriage is in the balance
unless his wife has an abortion. If she resists having an
abortion, suggest that he flat out threaten to leave. He can
tell her that she has no right to have a baby when he isn't
ready and add that, if she insists on going ahead, it will be
entirely her own private project. She will imagine herself
with a child but without a partner and that will certainly give
her a major case of what humans call "the cold sweats."

As always, pay careful attention to terminology. In the
arguments that are about to take place, encourage your
client to abstain from words like "unborn baby" or "unborn
child"—far better refer to it as an "embryo" or a "fetus." It's
amazing how useful a Greek or Latin word can be in filling
the human mind with fog while making the person
pronouncing such words feel more intelligent. As much as
possible, avoid the word "abortion." While it is better than
speaking of killing her unborn child, still "abortion" is too
sharp-edged a term and sets off various alarms. Plain words
often tend to be morally charged. Better to say "terminate
the pregnancy."

There is a battery of phrases that can help make abortion
more acceptable. I recall one client who always claimed it
was "just a clump of cells" she had gotten rid of. It never
crossed her mind that she too, even at age twenty-five, was
also just a clump of cells, only more of them, and would be a
clump of cells until her dying day. In fact "a clump of cells" is
an excellent definition for human beings in general. Why
the Enemy should be so attached to these clumps of cells has
always been beyond me.

No doubt you are aware that the Bible your client's wife put
on the coffee table asserts that these clumps of cells are

"made in the image and likeness of God." How absolutely nauseating. Our Enemy has the most astonishingly bad taste.

The point is that many battles are won or lost in the choice of words. If people are asked if they approve of killing unborn children, the answer they tend to give is not the one we care to hear—for most humans, the word "child" still has a halo around it. But if you ask if a woman should be deprived of "the right to choose" whether or not to give birth, even though the reality described is the very same, the answer is often quite different. A slight shift in vocabulary, a tweaking of emphasis, and suddenly the advocate of abortion is no longer advocating killing but is a defender of freedom.

Time and again I have seen people very nearly stride off in the wrong direction but do an abrupt about-face because the insertion of the right word or phrase, the right slogan, threw their conscience off balance. The majority of human beings will take pains not to *steal*, but if they can convince themselves that they are only *borrowing* something, albeit without the owner's awareness or permission, they feel it isn't a criminal act after all. And if the borrowed item isn't returned, that's only absent-mindedness. It crosses their minds that probably the owner hasn't missed what was borrowed and, if he has, is probably glad to have it off his hands. In the end, your thief will convince himself that he has done a good deed.

But to return to your present situation: Remember you are not the only spirit whispering in your client's ear. There is also the so-called "guardian angel" whose activities are as ceaseless as your own. You can take it for granted that your opposite number will be pointing out that abortion is the intentional killing of an innocent person—in a word, murder. In cases like this one we must help our clients center their thoughts on the fact that terminating a pregnancy is perfectly legal and drive home the idea that only religious fanatics oppose abortion while all sensible people recognize it as a fundamental human right.

In your next exchange with the wife's guardian demon, kindly pass on my advice that she should be made to feel as alone as possible, as isolated as someone stranded on a remote island the size of handkerchief. It's a point that won't need to be knocked in with hammer blows. The more alone and abandoned your client's wife feels, the easier it will be for her to make the decision that this is no time to have a child and thus take the step of killing it. We must promote the word "choice" and the phrase "better timing" while doing all we can to move humans toward choosing death and doing so with an overwhelming sense of choicelessness.

Warmly yours,

Wormwood

Wormwood Message 9

TO: Greasebeek

FROM: Wormwood

SUBJECT: Play plus boy

My dearest Greasebeek,

Drawing your client's attention to the population explosion documentary on CNN—that was resourceful of you. If you can keep him on this track, he will soon convince himself that, far from being evil, abortion is a sad but necessary social duty, required for the good of the human race and the protection of the planet. He will come to see it as an act of moral courage, and conclude that anyone who avoids parenthood in this over-populated day and age deserves a medal.

Still, the tide doesn't seem to be turning your way, does it? His wife didn't respond in the manner one would have wished. You mention her comment that she doubted the film's producers actually liked children and that they seemed more worried about too many poor people than too many babies.

One needs no crystal ball to see that your client's wife is more and more determined to go ahead with motherhood, ready to do so even if she has to do it entirely on her own. If only she had kept her pregnancy secret a little longer! Then there would never have been all that sympathy and enthusiasm from friends and co-workers or offers to help if her husband walked out. Even your client seems not altogether sold on the necessity of abortion. Am I correct in guessing that he has withdrawn the threat of divorce?

There was also her disturbing remark that husbands are easier to replace than babies and that abortion fits right in with "the Playboy philosophy."

I take it your client has a stack of *Playboys* or some similar journal hidden away in the bedroom? It has never been entirely clear to me why magazines featuring photos of naked females are so popular. No doubt this blind spot has to do with our being bodiless while human beings are—to put it bluntly—so physical. On the other hand, it impresses me that magazines with such photos only have a certain *type* of naked women in a certain narrow age range. It isn't only skin blemishes that are removed. One never sees any babies in publications of this type. One never sees pregnant women. The message is clear: sex without promises or consequences.

In interesting word, *Playboy*. Play. Boy. A pair of words made one. A term for a mature male (if only in terms of physical development) remaining in an ongoing artificial childhood. A permanent boy in permanent play. Nothing about work, no suggestion of becoming a man. Instead, he is encouraged to live as long as possible in a sexual fantasyland.

Speaking of which, what about your client's use of the Internet? I find it odd that there is very little in your reports about what he doing when he is on the web. Is he visiting pornography sites? If not, why not? Especially now, with his marriage under strain, every effort should be made to turn his fantasy life toward images of other women—younger women, more willing women, women who are sex objects and nothing more, or at least are made to seem so. I realize you find this whole area of human activity disgusting. Be assured that I take no pleasure in thinking about such matters, still less in writing about them. But I can tell you from long experience that this is an area of human life where downfalls come easy.

To the extent that he can be made to regard women in general mainly in physical terms, he will become a more physical being. His interest in spiritual things will begin to wane, which is exactly the outcome we want.

Yours warmly,

Wormwood

Wormwood Message 10

TO: Greasebeek

FROM: Wormwood

SUBJECT: Temptation and guilt

My dearest Greasebeek,

I'm delighted with the headway you are making on your client's use of the Internet. You were right about using "erotic art" rather than "pornography" as a key phrase. In essentials both often mean the same thing, but the word "pornography" is sometimes too straightforward. Your man is clearly the sort of person who wants to regard himself as having a higher level of taste—not someone drawn to the crude photos that might appeal to an auto mechanic. No, he wants a better sort of sexual imagery, more artistic photos, though in fact what he is looking at may well be more degrading than any picture you might find on an auto repair shop wall.

There is of course nothing new about pornography. The sort of thing your client has been looking at on the Internet was available on the walls of many Roman houses two thousand years ago. Or consider Japanese pillow books. Or French postcards, so popular a hundred years ago. The factor that has changed is that never before has this kind of imagery been so readily available or obtainable without face-to-face contact with the seller. Once on the web, all that is needed are a few clicks of a mouse!

You ask if I would explain human beings and sex because you "find it so confusing." I must admit that, even after all these years in the temptation business, I still find this topic fundamentally bewildering. One can see at a glance that sex is a major feature of human identity. Indeed, it is apparently such for all material beings, though with ordinary animals it is on the whole a straightforward undertaking that has nothing to do with feelings, love, fidelity, or promises. But for the human being sex seems to have more than a procreative meaning. People long for stable, permanent relationships and often manage to overcome sexual temptations that would put their primary relationship at risk. Even so, one can see that sex is a subject very often in their thoughts—and notice that they too sometimes find sex just as odd as we do.

Given that we demons are associated in their thoughts with sexual temptation, if nothing else, those humans who believe we actually exist would be astonished that we have no interest whatsoever in sex and indeed are incapable of such an interest. Living entirely without sex is one of the great advantages of being a non-physical being. There has never been a monk more celibate than your most lackluster demon.

Yet even if we cannot experience *sexual* lust, we understand lust quite well. We know what it is to want to own someone, to utterly possess him, to have charge of his activities, to know exactly what he will do the way a puppeteer knows how his puppet will perform. We know the hunger to dominate. And with this knowledge we can at least imagine an aspect of what happens to human beings when sexual lust takes hold of them.

Your client seems to be close to ordinary—heterosexual, no affairs during his marriage, no more than the usual interest human beings have in glimpses of the naked bodies of the opposite sex. No doubt there are many minor temptations he has given into and which he would bring to confession if confession were part of his life, but as yet there have been no headline items—what among Christians are sometimes called mortal sins.

Nevertheless, if you can manage to fill his mind with images of sexual activity, no matter how nauseating you find them yourself, and promote the idea that this is all entirely normal and healthy and ought to be indulged in freely, you would be amazed how his direction in life can gradually be shifted.

Little by little a parade of ideas will occur to him.

One is that, compared to many of the women he is looking at, his wife isn't nearly so attractive, even if in the past she may have seemed a miracle of beauty. Nor is she likely to be the insatiable sexual athlete he encounters in pornography, though of course in actual life the women whose photos he contemplates may enjoy sex a great deal less than his wife does. For them it is truly a job, if not slavery. But in their line of work, the appearance of pleasure is a necessary mask. Don't let him think about who these women actually are and what their lives are like.

What humans fantasize about becomes more and more what they think about actually *doing*, and with that comes a process of developing and embracing justifications. "Is it after all so bad to have"—I use a current phrase that has a useful clinical ring—"*multiple sexual partners*? Didn't men in the past often have many wives and concubines? Even in the Bible? Isn't this still the case in certain cultures? Can it be all that bad?" You can even give his thinking a religious twist: "God gave me all this sexual energy and appetite. God filled me with all these hormones. Surely God can't object to my doing what I am designed to do? If there is anything wrong in it, it's God's fault for making me this way." (But be on guard. His guardian angel will almost certainly attempt to point out that creation, and human beings with it, has been damaged by human sin. It's a basic tenet of Christian theology: the Fall of Adam and Eve, the exile from Paradise, etc. But this will seem a remote idea to your client, who probably thinks the book of Genesis is nothing more than a collection of ancient fables.)

If you work on this with patience, your man may arrive at a state in which situations where sexual attractions he would once have had the strength to ignore become so powerful that eventually he commits adultery.

At that point, you will find his mind alternating between excitement and guilt in rapid succession.

The trick then is to make him feel guilty about feeling guilty. Drum the message into him that guilt is neurotic, guilt is weakness—that sort of mantra. Here, once again, the times are with you. A great many people these days regard guilt as a mental illness. Sins are explained away in terms of family background, poor diet, communication problems, misunderstandings, genetics, and psychology. Indeed the human being today who so much as dares pronounce the word "sin"—unless in an ironic voice—is likely to find people around him searching for the exits.

But I am looking too far ahead. So far your client is only at the picture-gazing stage, and not very far along in that. He takes pains to do it with the utmost secrecy. Embarrassed, yet fascinated, he is still far from actions that endanger his marriage or his soul.

You have your work cut out for you.

Yours warmly,

Wormwood

Wormwood Message 11

TO: Greasebeek

FROM: Wormwood

SUBJECT: Hurting no .one

My dearest Greasebeek,

At last some good news from you, though taking a female co-worker out to lunch several times falls well short of actual adultery. Still, this is a promising start. At this point the lies he has told his wife are a victory, as are of course the lies he is telling himself: "It's just a harmless friendship."

I gather he finds the lady quite alluring and, still more important, enjoys being regarded as attractive and fascinating by a woman several years younger than he is. His wife, meanwhile, is more interested in the child she is carrying than in him or anything else. No doubt he is feeling sidelined, neglected, taken for granted, emotionally abandoned.

He also has embraced the idea that spending time with his co-worker is something of a kindness to her—that she is having a difficult time adjusting to a new work situation and is in need of friendly advice from a welcoming colleague. Well done!

Resting his hand on her arm while they drank coffee yesterday, tiny and brief a gesture though it was, marks the crossing of a border of intimacy.

This is the moment to help him develop the thought that, even if things were to go much further, even if they were to end up in bed, they *wouldn't be hurting anyone*. That's your slogan. You will not need to be very inventive. Once a human being finds someone sexually attractive, he will come up with no end of justifications for translating thought into deed, and will tell whatever lies are needed in order to cover his tracks. He may even enjoy the adventure of secrecy. Ditto for women. These days they think and operate in much the same way.

How many times—but too late—have I heard a client say, "But I didn't mean to hurt anyone!" In my own case load, not long ago there was a man whose wife, once he admitted what he had been doing and owned up to the lies he had told her, killed herself. The man was absolutely bewildered because in his own mind he loved his wife as much as the woman he had been having an affair with. He had even expected to win points for "being so honest." My success in that case was partly due to keeping him from reflecting what he would feel if he were to discover his wife in bed with another man—the sense of betrayal that would have overwhelmed him. In his case, it might well have led to murderous rage. It would have meant nothing to him that she "didn't want to hurt anyone." But I managed to keep his thoughts focused entirely on his own desires, which soon enough became his irresistible needs.

It never ceases to amaze me how easily human beings can decide that whatever sin they are committing is harmless and that no one need ever know. They seem to think that if a stone is thrown into the water carefully enough, there will be no ripples.

Yours warmly,

Wormwood

Wormwood Message 12

TO: Greasebeek

FROM: Wormwood

SUBJECT: E-rage

My dearest Greasebeek,

I am more than disappointed to hear that your client has been taking care not to get closer to his female colleague— even showing her a photo of his wife and telling her about the child they are expecting. A pity. That relationship seemed to be shaping up so well.

Today's turn of events may be short-lived. Wait for a good sizzling argument at home. It's bound to happen. They seem to average at least one per week.

Equally disturbing is the news that your client has decided to "take more control" of his Internet activities and has even set up filters to block certain kinds of sites. It seemed to me that at last you were the one taking control. Please don't shower me with any more blather about how clever his guardian angel must be. The point is how *un*clever you seem to be.

I assume you have reported all this to your supervisor, my respected colleague Izdrack, or will very soon do so. In that regard, don't forget that my role is entirely just between the two of us and need not be mentioned in any report. Izdrack is a hot-headed type who might think my off-the-record assistance is to blame for your blunderings, and this wouldn't be helpful for either of us.

There is, mind you, another line of attack that might prove fruitful so long as your client remains involved in the Internet. You might urge him to sign up for an e-mail discussion group, perhaps one with a religious focus. Suggest to him that this will help in his spiritual development— questions answered, valuable discussion, good resources publicized, perhaps the discovery of some new friends on a similar journey. There is some risk in this strategy, as there are occasional discussion groups that have a peaceful and constructive character, but the majority are dens of electronic squabbling or worse. One sees a good deal of "e-rage" between people who have never met face to face, and who, were they to do so, might get along very nicely, but who turn into spiritual cannibals while firing messages back and forth with no greater obstacle than the send button.

E-mail has the great advantage of being a completely abstract medium: no eyes to look at, no tone of voice that gives words a different shade of meaning, no body language to decipher, not even a piece of paper that another hand has touched, folded, put into an envelope, and sent on its way. Nothing material! Just impersonal words on a screen. The process resembles dropping bombs from a great height; the pilot whose plane is a pinprick in the sky sees no bodies being torn to shreds, only quiet blossoms of flame.

While surfing the Net yesterday I happened on one e-mail discussion group where the topic happened to be the Virgin

Birth. One participant—one of my current clients—raised an objection to the term. How could anyone be so naive as to believe that a virgin, a woman who had had no sexual relations with a man, could possibly bear a child? How could the authors of the New Testament expect readers to accept such patent nonsense? He saw it as "a myth revealing a negative attitude toward marriage." (I don't mean to pat myself on the back, but I'm pleased at how things are going with my client. He takes pride in being a skeptic, which for him is a synonym for intelligence.)

There was a response from someone who said she believed in the Virgin Birth. "A God able to create being out of non-being and matter out of nothing surely can cause a woman to become pregnant if it serves a special purpose," the lady argued. This made me somewhat anxious, but then a third individual joined the discussion. He suggested that the pro-Virgin Birth woman was the village idiot and ought to read up-to-date theology. He explained how biblical scholars understand such "miracles"—he used quotation marks—as "meeting the psychological needs of primitive people." He blathered on for a time about how benighted people had been two thousand years ago before science turned on the light. "The Virgin Birth myth is one of many the New Testament texts which hide the historical Jesus within a shroud of legends." He went on to add that even more absurd was the idea that Christ had actually risen from the dead. "His ideas lived on—that's what the resurrection legend is really all about."

After that posting, the list in question had a great deal in common with the inside of a volcano. As of this morning, the lava is still flowing. A human being doesn't have to die to visit Hell. It can be entered via the Internet.

The "Christian Spirituality" discussion group is doing a world of good for my client. Not only has he become increasingly irritated, but he is more and more at home with sarcasm. This is becoming habitual not only in his e-mail messages but also in conversation with friends and colleagues. If his development continues along the lines I have in mind, sarcasm will become his default setting. He thinks it demonstrates how advanced his thinking is and shows that he is "superstition proof."

Why not bring the Christian Spirituality List to your client's attention? With a label like that, your whisper will not even seem like a temptation.

Yours warmly,

Wormwood

Wormwood Message 13

TO: Greasebeek

FROM: Wormwood

SUBJECT: Prayer in the trenches

My dearest Greasebeek,

You have admitted that your client went inside a church at
lunch hour two days ago, looked around, sat in the back for
fifteen minutes, and then got on his knees for a short time.
Did he make the sign of the cross? Presumably not, or you
would have mentioned it. Even so, you don't need me to tell
you that this is the kind of event that can signal disaster, and
not only for your client but also for yourself.

Your e-mail message is also curious in its failure to mention
anything about what your client was thinking about before
or after. Surely it wasn't all prayer or even chiefly prayer. Of
course I realize you can't overhear prayer. Sadly, our
scientists have not yet found a way to crack the code. It
would be so much easier to find the weak point if only we
could listen in (however unpleasant that might be).

Nonetheless, conjecture often helps. One might reasonably
guess that in your client's case the prayer is linked to his
wife's pregnancy. Panic will often get even the most convinced

atheist to discover in himself an overwhelming need to pray. People we had become altogether complacent about owning forever occasionally manage to break free of our direction at the last moment and escape, which has always struck me as absolutely unfair. There really are "deathbed conversions," even if they are a rarity. Fortunately, the older people get, the more attached they become not only to habits but to ideas. Nevertheless, there is no ignoring the phenomenon of prayer in the face of extreme peril—"foxhole prayer." It is always a danger, even in the case of people we have every right to feel secure about. I know from his Demon-in-Charge that even Stalin resorted to prayer when he saw death coming his way. In a pinch, the most hardened unbeliever may recover the hope that there is a merciful God in Heaven after all and make an urgent application for help.

Your response to this event was so passive that it seems you were in a coma-like state. What could you have done, you ask?

The simplest and often the most effective tactic is to let him picture himself at prayer, attaching to this image the question: "Would I want my friends to see me on my knees?" Until they get used to it, modern people tend to regard being seen at prayer as more embarrassing than a walk through a supermarket in their underwear. If you can pull a person's mind away from his prayer to simply picturing himself praying, you will have activated the embarrassment factor. I've seen it work countless times. Your client will glance nervously around the church to see if anyone is looking at him and, a minute later, relieved not to have been noticed, get off his knees and make his exit.

Speaking of exits, most churches usually have a literature rack near the exit. If you are lucky, one or more of the booklets may be narrowly sectarian—why Church A, the church he is visiting, provides secure access to Heaven, while Church B down the street is a major gateway to Hell. Disputes between Christians are an excellent way not only of keeping church members in a praiseworthy state of mutual contempt but also of confusing and scandalizing those who, like your client, are watching from the sidelines and trying to make sense of it all. Who would want to be part of a religion whose membership is so bitterly divided? So tribalized?

But this can be tricky. You must know your client before opting for this strategy. Avoid it in cases where a client shows an unhealthy interest in truth as such. The danger here is that it might cross his mind that truth implies non-truths, if not outright lies, and that a healthy church cannot pretend that lies don't matter or that heresies don't exist. While we have done a reasonably good job of making the word "heresy" unfashionable, or a word to be used only with irony, there are occasionally cases in which a client realizes that there must be substantial issues behind the fragmented state of Christianity.

I once had a case where, after months of things going the Enemy's way, the wind suddenly turned in my favor when the man in question discovered that the particular church to which he was drawn kept an eye out for heresy and didn't hesitate to refer to certain people as heretics. Luckily, for my client, "heresy" was an out-of-date term associated with inquisitions and torture chambers. He was shocked at how close he had come to joining a community that used such an antiquated word about the "sincerely held opinions of others."

As I understand your man, he is exactly that type, more interested in sincerity than truth. At least in this stage of his religious development, he will want to see all churches as being "basically the same" and find theological disputes of any kind bewildering and off-putting. His ideal imaginary Christian is tolerant, if nothing else. He will regard not only the varieties of Christianity but all religions, no matter how hugely they differ, as spokes on a wheel, with all the spokes converging on the same hub.

Sincerity is a kind of wallpaper that's useful for covering the ugliest cracks. People these days can be forgiven almost anything so long as they are regarded as sincere. For some reason it doesn't cross their minds that one would be hard-pressed to find people more sincere than Hitler or Stalin, nor does it occur to them that Hell (should they think about Hell at all) is crowded with people who committed sins in a state of absolute sincerity: sincere anger, sincere greed, sincere jealousy, sincere lust, sincere pride.

I wonder if you have any idea how fortunate you are to be at work in a culture in which the word "truth" is suspect. Your job is much easier than it was for so many of your prede-cessors. Truth in the current age is a word in quotation marks. Most of the people you are dealing with can use the word comfortably only in the plural. By all means let there be *truths*—the more, the better. I can relax when I hear someone say, "I don't agree, but I respect your point of view." It's a way of saying, "It doesn't really matter."

I had a priest client who became a bishop in his later years. The man could sing the creed with enthusiasm on a Sunday and on Monday devote himself to writing books denying the contents of the creed. He believed neither in Christ's virgin birth nor in his resurrection and made a name for himself by publicizing his opinions while denouncing as out-of-date those who believed the creed. Time and again he was asked, "How can you recite a creed you don't believe?" He would smile patiently and respond that the creed should be understood symbolically and poetically. Once you saw it as a poem, once you understood that "virgin birth" and "resurrection" were metaphors, the actual words posed no problem. As he liked to say, "The church has space enough in it for everything but dogma."

I nearly lost him toward the end of his life when it crossed his mind how much being seen as up-to-date had meant to him and what a dangerous thing it is to want to be regarded as modern, but he knew he couldn't bear the embarrassment that he would have to endure if he were to deny what he had written. It was finally the fear of looking like a fool that kept him where we wanted him.

Warmly yours,

Wormwood

Wormwood Message 14

TO: Greasebeek

FROM: Wormwood

SUBJECT: Free-range fish

My dearest Greasebeek,

You mention—in small print, as it were—that your client has again slipped into a church. Please don't suggest that he was simply seeking shelter from the rain during his lunch hour. Clearly your client, a very worried man right now, is increasingly succumbing to temptations to pray. In fact, you admitted that he put a candle before an icon and got down on his knees.

You can console yourself with the reasonable conjecture that so far it's probably only *conditional* prayer. Many people engage in conditional prayer and never go a centimeter further. There is rarely any rooted belief in such desperate outbursts and little if any actual love for our opponent. Actually, this kind of prayer can easily turn in our favor. It boils down to saying. "Do what I want and then I'll believe you exist. Maybe." If they don't get what they want, and quickly, they are in the end better atheists than ever. They seem to think our opponent either isn't there or isn't worth talking to if he doesn't behave like a submissive Santa Claus.

The fact that your client hasn't mentioned these episodes of prayer to his wife or any of his friends is a good sign. It suggests not so much modesty about praying—not at all useful to us—but anxiety about what others will think.

Nothing is more threatening to our ends than genuine prayer. So long as it lasts, it involves an absolute loss of contact and power.

At this juncture, your best line of attack is to seed his mind with the thought that prayer is something done by stupid people. Smart people are self-reliant. Smart people find solutions themselves. Smart people make things happen. Smart people do not believe in what they cannot see. Smart people don't talk to invisible beings. Smart people don't do stupid things.

You are fortunate to be at work in a culture in which most people would far rather be regarded as wicked than stupid. Our Enemy is known to have remarked that the pure of heart are blessed, but these days people would far rather be blessed with high-power brains. Let pure hearts go to the stupid people. Blessed are the brilliant!

In an age like the present one, we can only be grateful that human beings are more socialized than a school of fish yet fail to perceive how carefully they tailor themselves to conform to the expectations and attitudes of others. While conforming in every essential way, they imagine themselves to be independent, autonomous, emancipated free spirits, mavericks, loners, etc. You will hear a New Yorker sneer about tribalism in Brazil while the thought will never even cross his mind that no one between the north and south poles is more tribal than he himself is, that his clothes and social behavior are as inherently odd as face paint and dancing to drums in a remote corner of the Amazon basin. No matter where they live, what they wear or don't wear, what ideas they claim as their own, what slogans they recite, these are tribal creatures. Happily, however, many of them don't think so. That is why Marlboro cigarettes have been so popular—all those ads of solitary cowboys on horseback in the middle of nowhere. Despite dire health warnings and the ever-rising cost of cigarettes, the company that makes them sells millions of packs every day to people who like to think of themselves as individuals!

Do you now begin to glimpse what our higher-ups are doing and why it's only you small fry who are assigned as guardian demons? The task of senior demons is the creation of useful social currents. Once an idea or activity of the right sort has been made fashionable, rivers of people are ours with only the slightest effort. Long before the first billboard went up, Our Father Below was well aware that it pays to advertise.

Still, even if people are as easily herded as sheep, we need sheepdogs like you to make sure they don't wander into cathedrals, light candles, kiss icons, and start praying. I don't envy what will become of you if you don't do a better job of tending your particular sheep.

Yours warmly,

Wormwood

Wormwood Message 15

TO: Greasebeek

FROM: Wormwood

SUBJECT: Rush hour

My dearest Greasebeek,

Your passing remark about the new watch your client purchased last week has set me thinking about an angle of attack that you have neglected so far: the development of a more desperate sense of time.

One of the advantages guardian demons enjoy these days is that in the entire history of the human race people have never been more governed by time than they are today. Not many generations ago not even a king knew exactly what time it was, nor did he need to. Now a stock boy working in any supermarket can tell you it's seven minutes past three. Times have changed!

In countries that regarded themselves as Christian, it used to be that people's activities were coordinated by bells in church towers. Bells marked out the hours of the day as well as special events—marriages and baptisms, deaths and burials. One could learn all sorts of things from bells. Today, a world coordinated by church bells is nearly as remote as the world of dinosaurs. Indeed many modern people would complain about "noise pollution" if church bells were rung as in the old days.

Clocks, whether on walls or wrists, are machines that have immense power in the lives of today's people. Everyone past the age of thirteen has a watch and, by and large, it rules their lives. If they learn nothing else at home and in school, it's to be on time: on time for meals, on time for classes, on time for sports, on time for social events, on time for their favorite TV programs. Many people—doctors, lawyers, plumbers, auto mechanics—speak of their working time in terms of "billable hours." There is even a proverb that says "Time is money." It rings a bell with just about everyone.

The clock has actually become a religious symbol of secular society. On the wall in many an old building, the nail that once held a crucifix now holds a clock.

Yet, despite all this careful measuring of time, almost all people find themselves lacking time as never before, which is very favorable for us. You must hear it often enough from your client: "I haven't got time." But don't be misled. It may sound like a whine, but often it's a boast in disguise. It rarely happens that anyone seriously thinks there might be ways to be less busy or manages to be less busy for any length of time. Even their vacations tend to be busy affairs. Their minds are busy even when their hands and feet are still. It hardly crosses their minds that being busy is primarily a state of mind.

Your client is probably the sort of man who, when he finds he is running late, will drive over the speed limit or push his luck with a yellow light at an intersection. Whether walking or driving, if he happens to see someone in need, he won't pause to find out if he can help because either he is already late or he will be made late by stopping. Your job is to see to it that being on time is more important to your client than being a "Good Samaritan."

Speaking of which, you no doubt recall the story of the Good Samaritan from your study of Enemy Texts back when you were still in the Academy. Note the interesting detail that, before the Good Samaritan stopped to aid the injured man, two others had already passed by without stopping. These were what today would be called professional men— *busy* men, men in a hurry, men with no time for unplanned interruptions.

I take it that your client is as time-obsessed as most people these days, but you mustn't think he couldn't be more time-driven. If you coordinate your efforts with those of his employer's guardian demon, you may well find ways to put your client under more job pressure than is now the case. His impatience will steadily increase and gradually turn into chronic irritation. Let his work expand into his lunch hours and weekends and any temptations he might have to attend church services will evaporate. He simply won't have time.

This will also help us with the still unresolved issue of the unborn child. Your client can easily be made more anxious about the practical aspects of being a father and all the *time* parenthood demands. If he becomes obsessed with worry about losing his job, he will want to out-perform his colleagues so that, if anyone is let go, it won't be him. He will feel more time-driven than ever and at the same time be less and less available to his wife and, should she give birth, less available as a father. This in turn would bring on the sorts of tensions that in the short term favor abortion and in the long term trigger divorce.

Do your job well, plant the right thoughts and fears, and you will see that time is on our side! Just make sure he sees time as confining and rigid, not river-like, not flexible. Make sure worry has the upper hand. Keep his mind in a constant state of rush hour.

Yours warmly,

Wormwood

Wormwood Message 16

TO: Greasebeek
FROM: Wormwood
SUBJECT: Perfectionism

My dearest Greasebeek,

Here I am, thinking it is so much easier these days to point people in the right direction, that a guardian demon's life has become a bed of roses such as hasn't been seen since Nero was emperor, and you come along and show me that one minor demon's incompetence can undo every advantage your elders have gained for you. Such an easy case in such favorable times, yet you inform me that your client has abruptly "changed his mind" about abortion, definitely wants the baby, and has decided to "read his way through the gospels." Then you tell me that he and his wife went to a church service on Sunday and are wondering if baptism wouldn't be a good thing for their child and possibly for themselves!

If it were up to me, you would be taken off this case and given an appropriate reward for your ineptitude, a reward that would set an example for others of your rank, but there is the problem at present of finding a replacement. Your division manager, Izdrack, a great bore with no imagination, speaks of being shorthanded.

I note at least the absence of the usual "every-cloud-has-a-silver-lining" paragraph in your e-mail message. You finally seem to grasp the gravity of the situation and begin to imagine what would happen to you if your client died in a state of grace.

But there is no need to regard the situation as hopeless. Not at all.

I doubt you have looked closely enough at your client's response to the church service. Despite a few positive things he had to say about it afterward, there were certain unexpressed disappointments, if only about details. The music was not what he expected. (Actual choirs never sound like angelic choirs.) The service seemed a bit long—you noted that he stole a glance at his watch from time to time.

How much did he focus on the people around him? There are bound to be others in the church who dress or behave in a way that annoys him. Often there will be someone in the church the client already knows and actively dislikes—the neighbor whose house is painted an ugly orange, the mechanic who cheated him.

And what about the sermon? It will either have been too serious, and thus boring, or not serious enough, and in either event too long. Was he not let down?

You mention his remark to his wife that "Father John is not the brightest bulb" and "the word is out that he often wakes up with a hangover." We can take it for granted that your client assumes that any priest, given his office, should be exceptionally bright, highly spiritual, given to mystical experiences, and beyond reproach in his private life. Do whatever you can to put your client's expectations in high orbit, then let it gradually dawn on him that he is smarter than the priest and by and large a better person living a more ordered life. We may luck out and find Father John so disappoints your client that six months from now he will be joking about his "recent religious phase."

The main thing you need to do is let all his vague disappointments move to center stage in his mind. Let them trouble him like tiny splinters. The church is never, I promise you, never what people want it to be. Our best defense at this stage is perfectionism—"Yes, by all means, go to church, only don't settle for anything second-rate." Let your client attend services like a critic in a theater, watching for every false note, every complacent face, every dull moment, every crack in the wall, every hole in the carpet, every human fault, every lapse of taste. Do that, and it won't be long before he is safely out the door. And if he goes to another church? And another? So long as you can keep his focus on disappointing details, you need not worry.

You note that he has taken to visiting the religious section of a local book store. Normally I would never encourage anyone to read theology, but these days much that is labeled theology is written by people who regard themselves as experts on Christianity but who are not actual Christians. The books such authors produce cause us no alarm. Indeed, many can be actively promoted. If you can tilt your man toward the right author, he will begin to wonder if the New Testament isn't 90 percent made up, a literary creation produced by an early church with a product to sell and a dead body to hide. (Never forget for a moment that to humans, life after death, resurrection, the existence of a Creator, and so forth are far from obvious matters. A human being may easily come to think of himself as "intellectually brave" and "free from superstition" for rejecting such basic realities.)

What we have going for us is the simple fact that there are no perfect churches. Not one comes close to being what it aspires to be. Indeed, filled as they are by ordinary people, administered by ordinary people, how could churches be otherwise? Just don't allow your client to think along such lines.

Yours warmly,

Wormwood

Wormwood Message 17

TO: Greasebeek

FROM: Wormwood

SUBJECT: Theological argument

My dearest Greasebeek,

Finally you have sent good news: a theological argument! Husband and wife not speaking to each other! A feather in your cap!

You report that their argument was about sacraments. She thinks the bread and wine on the altar really "become the body and blood of the Savior"—therefore something to kneel in front of and regard with awe—while your client (to your credit) thinks the bread and wine "are merely symbols" and therefore not significantly different from what he had for lunch yesterday. Splendid!

I am reminded of those exhilarating centuries illuminated by inquisitors and stretch racks, when heretics were burned or drowned—the "Reformation" and "Counter-reformation" as they are known in history books. Each party regarded its splinters of truth as the whole truth. Each side was determined not to see anything admirable in an opponent, still less to admit that the other had the tiniest fragment of the truth. On both sides, love was replaced by rage, humility by self-righteousness, respect by contempt. The end result was Western Christianity blasting itself into ten thousand pieces like a bowl smashed on a stone floor. Still earlier on, a thousand years ago, there was the huge split along East-West lines—the "great schism." Now that was a time!

What all this means for you, you lucky demon, is that your client can't simply become a Christian but has to become a *variety* of Christian. Ah, but what variety? Here there are myriad opportunities, many ways of bursting your client's balloon. At this point he will be aware of three major strains from which he can choose—Protestant, Catholic and Orthodox. He will have certain ideas, certain preconceptions, certain prejudices about each of them. Then, as he starts looking closely at any one of them, he will quickly discover still more divisions—"liberal" and "conservative" factions, "high church" versus "low church," Lutheran versus Calvinist, evangelical and pentecostal, this ethnic flavor or that, and on and on. These days there are not only Protestants but also Neo-Protestants. If he is drawn toward Orthodoxy, then will it be Greek or Russian or Serbian or Antiochian or some other strand? In short, an infinitely complex maze.

While your client considers the complexities of the Christian maze you have a golden opportunity to altogether flatten his current religious enthusiasm. He will feel as bewildered by all the choices as someone trying to decide which of a thousand restaurants is best—and end up finding fault with all of them.

Perhaps our greatest triumph over the past twenty centuries has been our success in dividing, then subdividing and then sub-subdividing, the followers of Christ. Today one has the impression that there are more churches than there are Christians. We have managed to turn practically every sentence in their Bible into a battleground, with every battle producing at least one more church—and the battles still rage and the varieties of churches still multiply.

Your client's argument with his wife is a case in point. He dismissed the bread and wine on the altar as "merely a symbol." Indeed! Symbol is a word that has come down in the world. You ought to be grateful your man knows no Greek. Otherwise he might know what the word "symbol" really means: that which draws together. If he knew that much, then he might recall the word's antonym: "diabolic"—that which tears apart. This refers to us, of course, not a topic we want him to dwell on.

As you must have learned at the Academy, a symbol can be verbal as well as visual. Orthodox Christians still call their creed—the statement of belief they recite together during liturgies—"the Symbol of Faith." So far your client seems to have no interest in creeds. He may even find them distasteful.

But more often symbols are wordless. While these are numerous, the Christians' main symbol is the wretched cross. Keep in mind that this is not just a shape but, from the Enemy's point of view, a kind of map—a sign by which they remind themselves that they reach joy through sorrow. It is a way of declaring without words that resurrection involves dying to self, that to bear a neighbor's burden is the path to Heaven—all that sort of rubbish. I feel nausea in writing it down.

During Christianity's first few centuries, our strategy was to make the cross a scandal. What respectable religion would associate itself with a method of execution? What incarnate God would be so powerless—and make himself so unsightly— as to die in such a way?

In the current age we have concentrated on reducing the cross to the category of decorative jewelry, but so far we haven't been entirely successful in breaking the link with its actual meaning.

On the other hand, until recently your client would have been one of the many people who made no connection at all between the cross and Heaven. It was simply the sign of a certain religion. If he thought about it at all, perhaps he even saw it as a depressing death symbol. If so, you must do all you can to bring him back to that level of awareness.

Fortunately, most modern people think "symbol" is akin to a commercial logo, nothing more—not something real, not something to live by. If bodiless creatures like ourselves had blood, it would turn to ice at the thought of what that symbol has meant in people's lives in times past, and sometimes even now.

You must do all you can to keep your client's idea of symbols on the level of advertising. Every corporation these days has its own logo, none of which means anything, none of which has anything to do with truth. If he can see religious symbols as being like commercial symbols, your man will in the end become our meal.

To get back to the argument you reported: You seem to take comfort in the fact that your client is wrong and his wife is correct. But this is of little consequence. It could be the other way round. No matter, so long as each stays furious with the other and each regards the other as an imbecile.

Yours warmly,

Wormwood

Wormwood Message 18

TO: Greasebeek

FROM: Wormwood

SUBJECT: Which brand?

My dearest Greasebeek,

I am aggrieved to hear that your client and his wife were so readily reconciled. You have a remarkable gift for letting golden opportunities slip away from you. I am not convinced you notice your chance even when it is presented to you in gift-wrapping. I trust you are keeping in mind the price of failure.

Backing away from arguments and apologizing is, I regret to say, typical of humans. It's one of the most obvious areas of difference with ourselves. They also have an astonishing and irritating capacity for changing their minds. I have always found it extremely difficult to comprehend how the Enemy can have any respect for such vacillating creatures. Their views and opinions turn like weather vanes in gusty winds: one moment east, the next moment west. Very promising disagreements boil up between them; they glare at each other as if poised to commit murder—then an hour later are in each other's arms, apologizing, just like these two.

You can take a gram of comfort in knowing that your man probably hasn't actually changed his mind about the question that brought on their argument. While he hasn't said it aloud, he still thinks his wife entirely wrong and only regrets having gotten so angry over something that "after all isn't that important." The day may come when it dawns on him that there is an issue involved still worth arguing about, at which point I trust you will do a better job of keeping him on the right track. But, for the moment, the question seems to have become secondary.

To move on to the present situation, their "worsening Christian itch" as you put it: I agree that it is the child your client's wife is carrying, along with her determination to give birth, that has made both of them think in a new way about their future—what sort of "environment" their child will have, what sort of example they ought to set, what sort of people they should be, etc. They both seem to have shifted from fear of what having a child will mean to a loathsome condition of amazement. This is one of the very hardest attitudes to undermine. Your client takes pleasure in feeling the sudden movements the baby is making in his wife's belly. Your client's favorite word is "miracle." An alarming term.

You report that both husband and wife went to church together this Sunday and seem intent on going to yet another church next Sunday. Their current idea is "to explore the different forms of Christianity." Your client's wife has the notion that "it would be a good idea for the baby to be baptized, but where?"

You ask: What church would be least harmful? Which would be the most likely to "turn him off" Christianity?

It's true that some churches are easier for us to work in than others. Still, there is no church in which we haven't done quite well.

The churches that provide the easiest environment for our work are those that are most sectarian. These easily and often become whirlpools of bitter disagreement. If your client and his wife cannot be kept out of church, at least try getting them into a church that is more interested in denouncing error than in praising the Enemy. You will then find your task much less demanding.

One also has a warm spot for churches that regard belief in demons as old-fashioned. That makes our job much easier— human beings need not defend themselves against enemies that don't exist. No need for a raincoat if you don't believe in rain!

On the other hand, we do quite well in churches whose members are more fascinated with us than with our Enemy above. There are quite a number of churches more obsessed with Hell than Heaven. Many Christians are more interested in the number 666 than in the Trinity.

The really ancient churches in some ways present the hardest environment for successful endeavor by our operatives, but even in those contexts a resourceful demon is by no means fighting a lost cause. We have captured more than a few patriarchs and popes.

The bottom line is that you needn't worry too much about *which* variety of Christian he becomes, should he take that step. Instead, focus on getting him to develop a spirit of enmity toward all the forms that he chooses not to embrace. In Hell there is no shortage of people from all varieties of Christianity, and even here they still carry on their tiresome theological disputes.

Yours warmly,

Wormwood

Wormwood Message 19

TO: Greasebeek

FROM: Wormwood

SUBJECT: Zero moments

My dearest Greasebeek,

I can appreciate your desperation but I notice that it is
making you reckless. In such straits one needs not just a cool
head, but an icy one.

Your suggested that it might be timely for your client to see
you—in order, as you say, "to put the fear of Satan into him."
Clearly there are pages of the Tempter's Manual that you
ought to re-read, especially Section 12, subsection E, on
Apparitions. You will note that making a visual appearance,
while not altogether ruled out, is permitted only with the
agreement of your supervisor. Knowing Izdrack as I do, I am
confident that permission will not be given in this case. Even
he would see the folly in your resorting to such a strategy.

Perhaps I can best explain to you what lies behind the rule
by telling you of two cases where apparitions were permitted.

I recall a sixteen-year-old boy in California who seemed
entirely on the right track. His occasional experiences of

Christianity had left a mainly negative impression. He called himself an "agnostic," as it seemed to him a smarter word than "atheist." He regarded his occasional attacks of "God longing" as a childish weakness and viewed Christians as dull, bourgeois people, the opposite of what he aspired to. He used to frequent a certain book shop, our local missionary center, that had a fine section devoted to the occult and magic. He was fascinated by these books, never buying any but looking at them often, covertly, much the way on other occasions he looked at pictures of naked females. The idea of magic powers excited him. His stressful home situation was also in our favor: his parents were on the razor edge of divorce, entirely caught up in their own affairs, and the emotional climate of the house was cold yet potentially explosive. The boy felt lonely, isolated, an outsider in an absurd world. It was an ideal opportunity for us—what I call a "zero moment." For us there was the possibility of conversion to our cause. But, mind you, zero moments are also opportune for the Enemy.

His guardian demon made a request to appear and it was given. The actual event happened one night when the boy was walking near the ocean and had stepped into the ruins of a house that had burned down a year or two before. All that was left was a concrete floor and fireplace. The boy's demon, a spirit named Mandrake, found this an ideal location—after all, human beings associate abandoned houses with ghosts. Avoiding the spectacular, Mandrake appeared in a semi-human form, grey as ash, small as a twelve-year-old boy, lean as a dancer. He stood with his hands on his waist and laughed at his client—the usual "I own you and will own you forever" laugh that a demon can't help but feel when a client is on the right track.

It was a gamble—one has to gamble. I don't fault Mandrake for trying and it was all strictly by the book. Regrettably, in this case the results were not as we had hoped. Certainly the boy was convinced for the rest of his life that demons exist, and of course terrified, as a human being ought to be, but his terror had the wrong result. He didn't despair nor did he move further in our direction. Afterward he carefully avoided occult books—he never again entered that particular shop and ever after avoided any like it. Two years later he was baptized.

As the client is still alive, the story is not over, but we have at present little reason to be optimistic about the final result. No further appearances were permitted. In retrospect, it's clear we would have been better off had he been less certain that we exist. Of course the campaign is not over yet.

Another exception I recall involved a young man, nineteen at the time, an aspiring artist, very gifted, who was living in Paris. He had been drawn to the art and poetry of darkness— Rimbaud, Baudelaire, etc. He lived an ascetic life such as you might find on Mount Athos, though in his case it had nothing to do with devotion to the Enemy. Apart from his art, the driving force in his life was disdain toward those whose lives centered on such things as a fine meal, an excellent glass of wine, an expensive carpet—the sort of persons not in short supply in Paris. He harbored a praiseworthy contempt for his parents while remaining absolutely dependent on their support and living in their house.

He would have been an excellent catch. An experienced senior demon—I had better leave him unnamed—was assigned to his case and given permission to appear not once but repeatedly and to do so in all his magnificence. The young man had a model such as few artists ever dream of seeing: a being of cold beauty, pure power, and absolute intelligence, with dragonfly wings that shined like mica—a being the sight of which instantly reduces a human being to awareness of his utter nothingness. The young man was permitted to draw portrait after portrait. It was the best work he had ever done. One gallery put on an exhibition and it was well received. Everyone assumed these stunning drawings were works of imagination, since he said not a word about their having been drawn from a living model. By now his model had become his life, never speaking but often visible.

When at last the demon spoke, it was to say that this would be his last appearance unless the boy committed himself to our kingdom. It was a gamble to speak so plainly, but you must understand that this was a young man who was drawn to severe truths and abhorred any trace of sugar-coating. In any event, we regarded it as a no-lose arrangement—he would either agree or he would kill himself—for he was now absolutely dependent on his "showings," as he called them. He was living for his visions.

Given the ultimatum, he chose suicide. Unfortunately, he failed in the effort. After hours of walking the streets, he jumped into the Seine as a barge was passing, was knocked unconscious and was on the verge of drowning when some fool who happened to be passing dove into the river and pulled him to the embankment. Finding an address in the wallet, he managed to get him home and then visited each day, taking the young man for long walks that invariably included stops in churches where he would explain the stories imaged in the stained glass.

It was our double misfortune that the rescuer was committed to the other side and had no trouble believing the young man's story, assuring the parents that their son was sane and that he needed a rosary more than he needed a psychiatrist.

It is too early to say that our effort was in vain. The other side is correct in asserting, "Where there's life, there's hope." We also have our hopes! But the artist no longer despises his parents and never goes anywhere without his rosary. Occasionally he misses his "showings," but there are as yet no indications of his seeking their resumption. While we did indeed put the fear of Satan into him, it was finally replaced by that other kind of fear that I prefer not to think about, the fear that makes humans resistant to our promptings.

You might point out that your client is a different case and that, given his present instability, the shock of seeing you could lead him to put a gun barrel in his mouth, but we cannot count on it. It might only send him racing into church. Also bear in mind that even suicides are sometimes stolen from us. So much can happen in the soul even in the splinter of time between a trigger being pulled and a bullet tearing through the brain. What humans normally perceive as a fragment of time too small to measure can become a near eternity of time for the person who has pulled the trigger and is awaiting the bullet's arrival.

There is always the danger of clients repenting before death. They need only think the tiniest prayer of regret. Even beginning to say the word "mercy" seems to be enough. As you must know by now, the Enemy is without principle in accepting not only last-minute but even last-second conversions.

Yours warmly,

Wormwood

Wormwood Message 20

TO: Greasebeek

FROM: Wormwood

SUBJECT: Postcards from home

My dearest Greasebeek,

I was in a rush while writing my last message and had no time to deal with your question as to whether it might be useful for your client, if not to see you, at least to have "a less negative view of Hell."

What leads you to think he has *any* view of Hell? I mean actual Hell rather than preposterous images? It may be he was assigned a few cantos of Dante's *Inferno* in a world literature class in his student days. So what? Take it from me, no one in his classroom will have taken Dante's Hell seriously. *The Inferno* will have been described by the professor as "an exile's way of settling scores with Dante's numerous enemies in Florence" or, more broadly, "a glimpse into the dark recesses of the medieval mind."

Your client will have seen a thousand cartoon drawings about Hell, but the main effect will have been to make Hell as ridiculous as the Easter Bunny and flying reindeer. All that imagery of smoky caves and red devils with pitchforks does us no harm. No one need take seriously the idea that Forever really exists, still less the particular Forever we provide. If he thinks about Hell at all, it's in comic book images—jokes about the afterlife.

The essential thing is to keep him from noticing that Hell begins where he is, here and now, that entry doesn't require dying. This may also be true of Heaven, but in this regard one can only speculate. Death only closes the door of a room one has already entered.

Fortunately, their idea of Heaven is even more preposterous than their idea of Hell. The imagery used to be of clouds, harps, wings, and halos. In the current age it seems to have become a national park without mosquitoes, or a ticket-free eternal Disneyland that anyone who has been reasonably well behaved can enter—an everlasting vacation at life's end entered through a tunnel of light. What was once seen as a hard climb upward on "the ladder of divine ascent" from which many fell has now become nothing more taxing than a ride on an "escalator of divine ascent." The passive rider can relax; he need do nothing on his worry-free upward journey. (I admit that I know very little about the actual Heaven, nor wish to, but I know enough from their Bible to be aware that it has mainly to do with the desire to be in the Enemy's company and the Enemy's readiness to welcome them.)

To return to your question, leave him with whatever silly ideas he has about Hell. As they say: Better the devil you know than the devil you don't know.

Of course, I can appreciate the distress you felt when you discovered your client listening to a radio preacher ranting about how anyone who doesn't "accept the Lord Jesus in his heart" is doomed to everlasting hellfire. I have been obliged to listen to many such ranters for countless boring hours. I know their script better than they do. I do not claim that such remarks are entirely harmless, but in your client's case, while it may raise his blood pressure for half an hour, its main impact will be to make Christianity seem small and petty. Sooner rather than later it will cross his mind that an alleged "God of love" cannot be all that loving if there is no room in Heaven for Gandhi or, closer to home, the fifteen-year-old Jewish newspaper boy who was run over last week two blocks from your client's front door. Let your client think of our Enemy above as a near-sighted, bad-tempered border guard carefully checking membership cards at the pearly gates. What decent person would wish to be in such a heaven?

You can thank your lucky stars that the upstart from Nazareth's actual words about the Last Judgment—his nauseating principle, "what you did for the least person, you did for me"—are rarely mentioned by radio and television preachers. The "works of mercy" are not their theme. No need to feed the hungry or welcome strangers. What is of the greatest theological interest for many of them is the contents of the collection basket.

Yours warmly,

Wormwood

Wormwood Message 21

TO: Greasebeek

FROM: Wormwood

SUBJECT: War

My dearest Greasebeek,

I am amazed that you are so ecstatic about the outbreak of war, as if this were in fact a whirlpool that could unfailingly drag your client forever out of the Opponent's reach. If only it were that simple.

You write that your client is thinking seriously of joining the army and that you are doing all you can to "cheer him along" so that the idea becomes a firm resolve. I am not saying it would be a disaster if he joined the army, only cautioning that you mustn't assume that once he is in a military uniform things will inevitably go our way.

Granted, war tilts many things in our favor. The general who said "War is hell" wasn't a bad theologian. There is no human endeavor so merciless as war. Of its nature war makes killers of harmless, law-abiding people who formerly took care to stop at red lights. War also has the attraction of destroying many people long after the cease-fire is signed— consider the high suicide rate among veterans.

Not that suicide is the only measure of success. I enjoy most not those who can never forgive themselves for what they did in war but rather those who have lost all awareness that there is anything that needs to be forgiven. "I was only following orders," Eichmann explained at his trial in Jerusalem. Did you know he had nothing personally against Jews? Some of his best friends, etc. It was simply his duty to arrange the deaths of certain people, and what you do as a loyal citizen you must do with devotion. I know on good authority that he lost not even one night's sleep over his wartime activities. In such cases suicide is anticlimactic—a needless, untidy drama. He was simply a good German whose services the state could rely upon. He was genuinely puzzled. "How is it possible that anyone would wish to punish a man for being obedient? After all, it was war."

There is magic in the word "war." It creates a quality of unity and obedience that is rare in periods between wars. (I cannot say peacetime, which human beings cannot imagine.)

There are other advantages. In wartime few will seek to practice the Opponent's bizarre teaching to "love your enemies and pray for them." Even if they dare think of what such a teaching implies, to practice it during war would create far too many problems. There is the occasional Francis of Assisi, but such individuals are rare and are regarded as insane and unpatriotic. Admiration comes only after such people die and the wars they refused to join in are seen in the cold light of day. While war is being fought, any good deeds done to an enemy are likely to be seen as criminal, even traitorous acts.

War has the great advantage of distorting the way human beings *see* each other. War generates a kind of mass fever that makes it all but impossible for those afflicted to see anything good in whoever is designated as the enemy—in reality a people no less cared for by our Enemy than themselves. Often they are a people who used to be regarded in friendly terms and who, in the not distant future, may well become the best of allies. But for now they are perceived, to put it simply, as something like *us*, like demons, which hardly does justice either to them or to us.

But it must be noted that today one rarely encounters the pure, high-quality hatred that one could count on in former times. In this regard your client is typical. You describe his outrage while seeing a television report about the enemy's treatment of dissidents and prisoners and his imagining what he would do "to those bastards" if he could "only get them in his gunsight."

His response sounds promising, but the thoughts stirred up by propaganda may well prove a short-lived fantasy. If you look closely at your client's attitude toward his nation's current enemy, you will almost certainly be disappointed. Today's hatred is more like a tincture of enmity compared to what one would have found as recently as the First World War. In those days one could rely on people to swallow propaganda whole. Today they remain responsive to propaganda but at the same time are vaguely aware that to some extent—perhaps a large extent—they are being lied to.

Even in better times, when people were more trusting about government and the press, murderous hatred could in a matter of minutes give way to outbreaks of friendship on the most blood-soaked battlefield. During the First World War, where so much was in our favor, there was an appalling collapse of animosity one Christmas when soldiers on both sides sang carols together and had snowball fights! War hatreds in fact are not very personal and cannot be relied on once the soldier glimpses the face of his enemy and discovers someone very much like himself.

If your man were to join up, bear in mind that it is not at all a sure thing he will get anywhere near the battlefield, and, if he does, he is more likely even then to be in some support role than in actual combat. But should it happen that he is personally involved in killing anyone, we may find him farther from our grasp than he is while watching the war on a TV screen in his living room. If he kills anyone, it is less likely to be an act of hatred than a desperate effort to defend the lives of his friends or save himself. He may well feel miserable about the irreversible damage he has done to others and beg Heaven for forgiveness—which, bear in mind, is a request our Opponent tends to respond to positively. (Our role in such cases is to convince the client that forgiveness is impossible in certain matters and therefore should not be sought.)

In behavior, war brings nearly everyone, soldier and civilian alike, into extraordinary, almost hellish conformity. The average person, whichever side he may be on and whatever private misgivings he may have, is carried along by the powerful tides of his society and is likely to do whatever he is ordered to do, however appalling, as faultlessly as Eichmann. Yet even here one cannot be complacent. All too often one finds some corner of the client's heart which tends to be ashamed of what he is doing, a sense of horror about his role in the events in which he is taking part.

You mention, as if it were a positive factor, that war hugely increases the death rate wherever it occurs. Yes, of course, but never let it slip your mind that for us the decisive issue is not death as such, but rather the *state* of dying persons. In general it is best that they imagine death as something distant rather than close. It is when human beings are nose to nose with death that it dawns on them how trivial their lives have been, how so many of their activities were a waste of time, the extent to which fear rather than love governed their lives, how unfree they were—and the shock may move them quite suddenly in another direction. In the blink of an eye you find a man who year after year was the most determined atheist, a missionary of disbelief, having second thoughts. He used to regard those who prayed as sentimental fools and now, facing death, he discovers that it was he who was the fool. All too often we lose people we had counted on owning forever, and all because of the discovery of their own graves. It is the Ebenezer Scrooge Syndrome. War has a tendency to make them increasingly aware of our Opponent's existence. Where actual dying is going on, there tends to be more prayer, not less.

I recall the case of the Russian writer Dostoevsky. As a naive young man with a head full of idealist slogans, he got involved in a revolutionary society in St. Petersburg, was arrested, and was sentenced to death. He was within minutes of being shot by a firing squad when a horseman delivered a pardon from the czar. Conversion didn't happen on the spot, but little by little that close encounter with death made him into an unshakeable Christian. Even today the novels he wrote following his conversion do great harm to our cause. All this might have been otherwise if he had not looked down the barrel of a rifle when he was twenty-eight.

One more factor to bear in mind: War has the side effect of making people think of those around them with more urgency and care, even to the extent of being quite ready to die for others. It may be that the circle of care remains restricted—"the enemy" is excluded—but nonetheless the soul's diameter expands to include far more people than it did before. War on the whole makes those taking part less selfish.

A final suggestion to mull over: You may find that there would be certain advantages were your client to become a conscientious objector, so long as it is not undertaken with a motivation pleasing to the Enemy. Causes of any kind, even the cause of peace, tend to distance those taking part from actual people. There is nothing like manifestos and movements to get people arguing.

Today he may be daydreaming about joining the army, but there will be moments in the days and weeks ahead when, far from wanting to join the army, he will be horrified at the thought that he might become one of those maimed or killed and then start thinking desperately about how to avoid the risks of combat. At that moment, with a slight nudge from you, it may cross his mind that war is after all not something altogether good and that one way out is to take the moral high road. With good guidance, you may soon have him despising everyone in uniform and anyone waving a flag—each and every person who isn't doing what he's doing. You would be amazed at how a person who talks constantly of peace can be more a captive of hatred than any soldier on the front lines of war.

Yours warmly,

Wormwood

Wormwood Message 22

TO: Greasebeek

FROM: Wormwood

SUBJECT: Holy writ

My dearest Greasebeek,

I am sorry to hear that your client is reading the Bible in his effort to decide about how to respond to the current war. This suggests yet one more lapse on your part. On the other hand, with the right guidance, this need not be disastrous and might even prove helpful. There are so many books in the Bible, so many stories, such an avalanche of sayings, so many things that a modern reader can hardly understand or even imagine.

First and foremost, you must do your best to keep him away from the New Testament, because here the ground for confusion is much smaller. Luckily, the New Testament is at the back of the Bible. Assist him in thinking he must start at the beginning. In most cases that means he will read less than a hundred pages, decide that's more than enough, and decisively close the execrable book.

The problem with the New Testament, as presumably you learned in the Academy, is that it provides not the slightest

encouragement for killing anyone, or any sanction to despise
even one's worst enemy. Can you imagine? But in what
Christians call the Old Testament, there are entire wars that
are described as enjoying Heaven's blessing. Also you will
find numerous actions, some of which are not at all rare in
today's world, that are to be punished by death. Best to try to
get him to focus on that kind of material, because he will see
it as not only sanctioning war but also blessing enmity.

However, take care. Even in the Old Testament you must watch
a client's thoughts very carefully. Don't let your attention
wander for even the blink of a human being's eye. There are
many passages that are every bit as bad as the New Testament:
not fearing evil, rejecting death, choosing life, letting mercy
and justice embrace, walking undisturbed through the valley of
death, fleeing from all evildoers, commandments against
poisoning an enemy's wells or destroying his orchards, and on
and on. There is even a commandment not to kill. Be aware
that the more one reads of the Old Testament, the more one
gets into a swamp of mercy. Steer him away from the books of
the so-called prophets.

If, despite your best efforts, he persists in reading the Bible
and at last makes his way to the New Testament, hope is not
lost. We have enjoyed great triumphs even with those who
have memorized every verse in the New Testament. You
would be amazed to discover how even major themes of the
New Testament—love of enemies, mercy, forgiveness,
overcoming evil with good, hospitality to strangers, etc.—
have been explained away by Christian bishops and
respected theologians, not to mention cautious pastors eager
to please their congregations. Keep in mind that holding a
position of church leadership does not make a person
immune to war fever and local ideologies, especially when

flag-waving will benefit his ecclesiastical career. Without great effort, one can find Christian pastors blessing every sort of weapon, preaching the holiness of war, and calling down heavenly flames on whoever the enemy happens to be.

If you can turn your client's ear toward such voices, then he may come to understand the teaching he encounters in the New Testament as "ideals one must aim for but not necessarily put into practice here and now." Let him draw the line between ideals and actual life, with ideals floating above the earth like remote clouds rather than demands that might put him at odds with what society expects.

If need be, you can also remind him that many people now regarded as saints were soldiers. No doubt he will have seen images of some of them in church windows where they are shown wearing armor and bearing swords—people like Saint George fighting the dragon. Encourage him to think of George as a man for whom being both a soldier and a Christian was not at all problematic. Let him imagine that George was canonized because he was second to none in killing people rather than because he was an impudent young man executed for proclaiming his faith instead of pleasing his superiors by hiding it.

Take care, however, about the "dragon." That of course is a symbol for *us*, but with careful guidance your client will see it as evidence that Christians long ago were a simple-minded people who believed in monsters.

Yours warmly,

Wormwood

Wormwood Message 23

TO: Greasebeek

FROM: Wormwood

SUBJECT: Anticipate the quarry's next move

My dearest Greasebeek,

You say he has decided not to volunteer after all? This because of something he read in a newspaper about the killing of noncombatants? "Collateral damage," as they put it these days? Your client must have oatmeal between his ears not to have thought about this aspect of war before reading a journalist's description of the final minutes of a particular family caught in the crossfire.

You claim his recent bout of Bible reading had nothing to do with his decision, but I am not convinced. It is more probable that he is embarrassed to mention to friends that his decisions could be influenced by such a source. Like so many these days, he is the sort of man who would rather be seen reading a sex magazine than the Bible. (Isn't it amazing what human beings find embarrassing? And still more surprising what they fail to find embarrassing?) Thus he prefers crediting his actions to what he has read or heard via the news media than to anything that might lead friends to label him a religious fanatic.

I expect his wife may also have had a hand in his decision. With a baby on the way, she will not want her husband taking part in a war in a country neither she nor he can easily find on a world map.

Our hopes that he might be either a warrior or conscientious objector must be put on hold for the time being. However, you must stay attentive. Wartime always creates an emotionally volatile situation. With the right news event, the right slogan, the right social fever, a human being can do an about-face without hesitation or without even recognizing it as a change in direction. Perfectly calm, sensible people can suddenly become obsessed with national identity and do anything that is seen as patriotic. Level-headed people who seemed immune to all ideologies can from one week to the next turn into walking manifestoes.

You ask, "Why is it that human beings, in many ways so predictable, are prone to change their minds with little or no warning?"

In this they couldn't be more different from us, and the difference has been especially obvious in the past century or two. We demons know what we know and we stick to it. Human beings often seem like leaves that have been blown off a tree and fly wherever the winds carry them. This can often be to our benefit. In that regard, you younger demons have no idea how fortunate you are. It wasn't many generations ago that human beings were more often part of a church and tended to be more firmly rooted in their ideas.

Nonetheless, they have always been changeable in ways we can hardly fathom. What makes or breaks a guardian demon is his facility to anticipate shifts in direction and his resourcefulness in making good use of them no matter what.

Say your client is a nun famous for caring for the neglected. She cleans the wounds of dying people who smell like garbage. She sleeps on a mattress no thicker than a pancake. She prays hours a day. Even atheists regard her as a living saint. In such a case, a good guardian demon, while aware he is hunting a difficult quarry, will do his utmost to convince the nun that indeed she is a saint. He will help her look in the mirror and see her own halo. He will urge her to enjoy the praise she receives and encourage her annoyance that there are a few people here and there who regard her as a fraud. Perhaps in the end she will escape our net despite our best effort. Or perhaps not. The point is we never regard anyone as a lost cause until they breathe their last. Never.

How much less reason do you have to regard your client as a hopeless case. There is no danger of anyone regarding him as a saint. Far from loving his enemy, he barely loves his wife. He is currently reading a Bible that requires him to honor his parents, but his actual attention to them is minimal. The same book calls on him to love his neighbor, but in fact, according to your reports, nearly all his neighbors are strangers. It rarely crosses his mind to give anything away, and still less often does a charitable thought become a charitable action. You moan and groan about how difficult he is, while in fact he is nearly yours.

Warmly yours,

Wormwood

Wormwood Message 24

TO: Greasebeek

FROM: Wormwood

SUBJECT: Self-esteem

My dearest Greasebeek,

It pleases me to hear that your client is reading a book on self-esteem. Well done!

Allow me to boast. I take some pride in having played a role in the conversion of the terms "selfishness" and "self-centeredness" to "self-esteem." The old terms were seen as negative, even reprehensible. Few regarded them as compliments. "Self-esteem," on the other hand, has come to be regarded as something any healthy person should have as much of as possible.

It was before your time that the self-esteem movement came into being. I recall a book in the seventies that sold in the millions—*I'm Okay, You're Okay*. It was an early gospel of self-esteem. You might wonder why people who are "okay" would need a book to tell them so. Doesn't the existence of such a book suggest that perhaps human beings are not, after all, entirely okay? That there might be an *itty bitty* problem?

In the past few decades there has been a torrent of books, magazine articles, and television programs reminding people that, to the extent that they lack self-esteem, they will be unhappy, their marriages will be doomed, their careers will be stunted, while a society whose citizens are blessed with high levels of self-esteem will be more stable, more prosperous, and less troubled with anti-social or criminal behavior. Not many years ago, in the American state of California, the legislature was so convinced of the benefits of self-esteem that they created the California Task Force to Promote Self-Esteem and Personal and Social Responsibility! I kid you not.

It's true that a slightly more critical attitude toward self-esteem has emerged lately. Studies here and there indicate that self-esteem isn't delivering on its promises. One study found that people whose sense of self-esteem is based on good looks, favorable reception by others, academic or vocational achievement, recreational performance, or similar yardsticks are actually more at risk of relationship conflicts and aggression as well as more likely to become addicted to drugs or alcohol. Another group of researchers discovered that criminals rate particularly high when tested for self-esteem. And they were surprised by this! These surveys generated a few headlines.

Still, you need not be alarmed. The critics of self-esteem have so far had little impact. Few people will have heard of these studies. Among those who have, the majority will shrug them off. Self-esteem books sell well. Self-esteem seminars are well attended.

The more a person focuses on himself or herself, the better. If you want to love someone, love yourself. By all means be obsessed with external markers of self-worth: money, recognition, promotion, a better-than-average standard of living. Self-absorption is the key—the belief that personal success and happiness are of paramount importance. Let them think that "everything is about me," that there is nothing bigger that they need be concerned about.

Human beings want to be happy. There is nothing we have yet discovered that can remove that longing. But if we can help them embrace the idea that happiness is the consequence of achievements and possessions, we will be doing our job.

The Enemy has quite a different message about happiness. It is summed up in the text called "the Beatitudes," which I assume you studied in the Academy—"Happy are the poor in spirit, happy are they who mourn, happy are they who hunger and thirst for righteousness," etc. However, most Christians write such passages off as *ideals*, not something related to the normal lives of normal people.

In your client's case, now that you have him reading the self-esteem book, you have a golden opportunity. It may be that what was motivating his interest in Christianity was the expectation that in one way or another it would make him happier. Pose the question: But has it? Let him ask himself if in fact he hasn't become *less* happy in the months since his Christian quest began. Does he not look at himself more critically? *Too* critically? Has he not become more troubled? Isn't this religious quest of his backfiring?

His guardian angel will no doubt respond that a change in the direction in one's life is necessarily a painful, troubling business and remind him that the primary Christian symbol is the cross, not the featherbed. But what most humans are looking for—and your client is surely no exception—is happiness obtained in the easiest possible manner. No cross, thank you. No repentance either. Your side of the argument is the easier to win.

A human being can be carried along for years by self-esteem material, but sooner or later he will find himself on a dead-end street. The self cut off from others is in fact infinitely boring. In reality no human being, not even hermits, can exist without assistance from others. Human being are designed to find their main interest and fascination in others. The self exists only in the context of what Christianity calls communion. The Enemy's idea is to draw people ever more deeply into communion because only in communion can love and all that love implies be found. It is nauseating to contemplate.

If you do your job well, by the time your client discovers he is on a dead-end street, he will be in a condition of profound despair. His self-esteem will have become self-loathing. Bored and disgusted with himself, he will decide there is nothing to believe and no reason to live, period. At that moment suicide might will seem a reasonable, even necessary action. There is, after all, nothing. Existence is a sick joke, Heaven a myth. To keep living is to pretend that life has meaning. Better not to play that game but rather to pull the curtain down on the absurd farce of living.

Yours warmly,

Wormwood

Wormwood Message 25

TO: Greasebeek

FROM: Wormwood

SUBJECT: Icons

My dearest Greasebeek,

A pity your client threw away the book you had him reading. You could have chosen a better book for him. In this case the author's transparently anti-Christian attitude forced your client to recognize that he had a choice to make. To follow the route the author proposed would require abandoning the Gospel. This was too dramatic, too absolute. If only he had been reading a book that sought to reconcile self-esteem with the New Testament, you might have had a more positive result, even though it could have taken longer. In brief, you botched it.

For future reference, I will send you a list of books that argue—on biblical grounds—that before you can love anyone else, you need to love yourself. The authors point out that the Bible says: "Love your neighbor *as yourself.*" They interpret these last two words to mean that you have Heaven's blessing to make love of self the starting point, saving love of neighbor for some ever-receding future moment. It is an amazingly thin argument. I have read the Bible carefully many times. I can tell you with certainty that no one mentioned in the Bible who put love of self ahead of love of neighbor is regarded as admirable. Even so, Christian self-esteem books exist and are even sold in Christian book shops.

I have a client who thinks of herself as a Christian and who is forever asking her friends: "What have you done for yourself today?" When she dies, perhaps that sentence will become her epitaph. She is always annoyed when she finds people neglecting their own needs in favor of someone else's. She has a magnificent gift for making others feel guilty about not being more self-absorbed.

To get back to your client: The damage is done. One must let the dust settle and hope that another opportunity presents itself. For the moment, he seems sick of the term "self-esteem."

It is profoundly disturbing to read in your latest report that your client received an icon as a gift from a friend. What friend? What do you know about him? What steps have you taken to put an end to this unhelpful friendship?

You seem to take satisfaction in the fact that it is not a real icon, only a paper print mounted on wood, but I can assure you that paper icons can be just as dangerous as those painted by hand. All such images—the face of Christ, his mother, his resurrection, various "saints," scenes from the Bible, etc.—have the effect of encouraging belief and prayer.

In the West, icons were generally thought of as primitive art: flat, wooden, severe and lifeless. Regrettably, that attitude has been changing in recent years. The very qualities that long made icons objects of scorn now are viewed in a new light: the intentional flatness is seen as akin to modern art, the stillness as communicating a refreshing silence, the absence of smiles as an antidote to living in a society in which smiles are obligatory and often mask commercial or political strategies.

Nonetheless, you must not assume your client has had any access to these more positive views of icons. Indeed, he probably hasn't. He will be used to images that are more in the tradition of illustration or decoration. He will surely have noticed that there are a few icons in the museums he has visited and that these mainly serve as a starting point for real art. Encourage the idea that icons are the kindergarten of art and have little value for those who have left kindergarten behind.

Remind him of the idea often found in books of art history —icons were "Bibles for the illiterate." "Illiterate" is a word often taken to mean "stupid." But your client is not illiterate. He takes pride in the fact that he owns books and even reads them. He takes pride in his education. Let him think of whatever he has always been told is fine art and then compare that with icons. Let him be annoyed with the strange lighting, a lighting that comes from within rather than from an external source; the strange perspective—a vanishing point in front of rather than behind the image; and, finally, the uncomfortable stillness of icons.

Icons have their own language and, like every language, it must be learned—never an easy task! We ourselves are deaf to it, but we know from observation that it is a language mainly of silence—not an easy language for people who tend to find silence nerve-racking. This puts the situation in your favor.

Yours warmly,

Wormwood

Wormwood Message 26

TO: Greasebeek

FROM: Wormwood

SUBJECT: Victimhood

My dearest Greasebeek,

Your latest summary of the case gives many reasons for dismay, yet I note one area where I sense a vulnerability in your client that cries out for attack.

You report that your client's parents failed to send him a birthday gift and that this re-ignited painful memories about what he regards as a degree of parental neglect when he was a child. It is interesting that he should have told his wife that he grew up "a semi-orphan" because both his father and mother "were so busy with their careers." He sees himself as "a victim of bad parenting."

Along similar lines, you note that he was passed over for a promotion he was counting on and is furious that the job went instead to a female colleague. He is convinced he is "a victim of reverse discrimination."

In both matters, note that the key word is "victim." For the moment, at least, he is feeling like a victim both within his family and at his work place. This is your window of opportunity.

From the days of Adam and Eve, human beings have always had many things to be irritated about, or worse, in looking back on their years of parental dependence. The biblical commandment that human beings must honor their parents exists because even in the ancient world these creatures so beloved of our Enemy were often inclined to *dis*honor their parents.

In fact, if one thinks of what today is called "quality time," in those days children often were better off. In earlier ages a child would normally have ready access to at least one parent at any hour of the day or night. In those days no one worked in factories or offices. No one commuted. The father and mother had plenty of work to do, but it was close at hand and interruptions were always possible when needs arose. Young children would in fact work side by side with one or the other parent. Also, grandparents were far more likely to be nearby. All these factors tended to make for strong, multi-generational family structures. Parents and children might sometimes be at odds with each other, but there was rarely any question of neglect. Yet, even then, honoring one's parents was a major challenge to the majority of our clients—and many failed.

Since the "industrial revolution" the objective situation has changed radically. The family farm and similar intimate family businesses and trades have by and large disappeared. First men and more recently women have been forced to work away from their homes and apart from each other. In the case of women, there are countries in which this is viewed as "liberation."

Another change in the same period has been the development of institutional schooling. For many millions of children, schools have become an alternate home for a large part of the day—an environment as factory-like as the workplaces in which parents find themselves: clock-dominated, stressful, and impersonal.

In brief, your client, like nearly everybody, has a great deal to be angry about—memories of exhausted parents struggling to keep their jobs while he was a child, and now his own unhappiness at finding himself in similar circumstances, working at a job he doesn't like with people who raise his blood pressure.

The sense of being a victim is already there, if at present only sporadically, but with your encouragement this can grow into a state of full-blown victimhood.

You have access to his imagination. Help him imagine that, if only he had been given better parents, if only he had gone to better schools, if only he had landed better jobs, he might have become a happy person, but instead he has been hopelessly and permanently damaged by others and has a right to respond to life with anger.

At the same time, always try imagine what your opposite number will be up to when such an attack is noticed. With regard to your client's parents, it is not hard to guess that his guardian angel's message will stress compassion and forgiveness. He will argue that they did their best and that their human failings must be forgiven. Can you not hear it? The message will be something like this: "You see in your own daily life what they were up against and how tired you yourself are at the end of a work day. Think less about their shortcomings and focus instead on how well they did given all the difficulties they faced." Etc., etc.

As for his work situation, his guardian angel will surely be reminding your client that the traits he perceives in his colleagues perfectly describe his own traits, that he is no less competitive than they are, that apparent acts of friendship on his part are in reality thinner than wallpaper. Even if there are some shark-like people in the office, what can he expect in a damaged world?

Your client seems at this stage to see himself as a kind of outside-the-church Christian, a common breed these days. He has read the Sermon on the Mount and, as you put it, "been impressed by it." But you can take comfort in how little it has actually influenced him. Far from loving his enemies, there is no evidence that he would do any of them a good turn, much less pray for them. (Never forget that, bizarre as it sounds, one of the major duties of Christians is to pray for their adversaries. Happily, so far as we can tell, that sort of prayer seems extremely rare in actual practice.)

Don't be fatalistic. True, you have repeatedly failed in other lines of assault. But don't feel you have little chance of success this time. Victimhood is an area where the social tide is running strongly in our favor. It is a major growth area. In one way or another, all people can find a way of perceiving themselves as victims and can develop a sense of being obliged to resent—and even hate—all those whom they see as responsible for the damage but also everyone who seems indifferent to their variety of victimhood.

Assuming his guardian angel isn't asleep at the wheel, it will cross your client's mind that, as an aspiring Christian, he is

required to forgive. He will be reminded of this principle
each time he recites certain prayers—"forgive me as I forgive
others" and so forth. You may be lucky. It may be that the
real meaning of such words—a direct appeal to be forgiven
only insofar as one pardons others—hasn't actually dawned
on him and perhaps never will.

Should he begin to think along these dangerous lines, the
best strategy is to suggest that forgiveness is a wonderful
thing in general, but is out of the question in situations such
as his own. In any event, why forgive people who have never
asked to be forgiven? (They rarely do.) Or, if by any chance
anyone should ask for pardon, assist him in deciding it's too
soon. The wounds are still too fresh.

Impede in whatever ways you can any reflective process that
might lead him to see what he has suffered in life either in
structural terms or as the result of living in what Christians
are supposed to think of as a fallen world. Fortunately for us,
humans rarely recognize that the world is ideal for no one,
that no human being is unwounded or free of suffering.

Victimhood can become the defining core of identity, a
sweet reminder of Hell: so many people crowded together,
yet each of them so utterly alone, each a prisoner of rage.

Yours warmly,

Wormwood

Wormwood Message 27

TO: Greasebeek

FROM: Wormwood

SUBJECT: Rights

My dearest Greasebeek,

I am delighted with the news that your client has joined a local chapter of Victims Without Borders. You begin to show promise.

Be aware, however, that there are dangers in this strategy. I gather that the main idea of Victims Without Borders is that members gather once a week to listen to each other's painful memories and offer mutual support—not in principle something we would normally encourage. There is the danger that in such a setting your client could become overly concerned about what others have suffered and realize that in comparison his own problems are hardly worth mentioning.

Your major task must be to assist him in developing the counter-virtue of impatience. Specifically what is needed is a hypersensitivity to others talking too much about themselves. Let him become gradually more self-centered by becoming increasingly irritated with the self-centeredness of others. So long as he listens to others in an annoyed state, he will hardly be listening at all and thus compassion will not be given a foothold. Let him feel annoyance that the spotlight of group interest falls on him too briefly.

This is the ideal time to build up a certain passion for rights. The word "rights" has quite a good and wholesome sound to it and will provide him with the illusion that he is advancing the human race. Let him picture himself as a champion of "human rights" so long as the rights he is most concerned about are either his own or at least limited to his particular social segment.

A strategy that works in many cases and that might well be useful with your client, given that a promotion he was seeking went instead to a female colleague: Drum home to him the thought that he is a victim of the women's liberation movement, that men's rights are being eroded, that men are being marginalized, that women in the workplace are his enemy. All this can be reinforced if he finds his way into the company of misogynist men.

With those whose profiles are slightly different from that of your client, a tactic that sometimes works well is cultivating embarrassment about being male. One can develop a type of man who is more feminist than any female, who regards men as inherently violent, aggressive and oppressive, a type of man who regrets being born a male and who desperately wants to edit out of himself what he regards as male traits. He becomes radically at odds with himself, the bitter prisoner of his own anatomy and chromosomes. He will see himself and other men in fundamentally negative terms. He will find himself in a permanent state of anger that may gradually evolve into despair.

Whatever the variations that work best for your client, he should be thinking that from childhood up to the present day his rights have been violated—by his parents, by his teachers, by his employers, by politicians, by the structures of society. This is not hard. Indeed, probably they have been.

By the way, has your client had any unfavorable encounters with the clergy? Abuse of any kind? This could be another area of both victimhood and rights violation—indeed, it is hard to top. It would provide a solid basis for developing a rock-solid antipathy to any and all churches. Still, one can gather there were no major incidents along these lines or he would not at present be so well disposed to Christianity. A pity.

Speaking of this, is he persisting in attending Sunday services? Still sampling different forms of Christianity? Which churches? Is there a pattern to what churches he visits and his response to them? Is there any one church he is returning to a second or third time? What has he done with the icon he was given? Is he still reading the Bible? Your last report seems to me suspiciously lacking in essential details.

Yours warmly,

Wormwood

Wormwood Message 28

TO: Greasebeek

FROM: Wormwood

SUBJECT: Saints

My dearest Greasebeek,

You see how one thing leads to another? Allow the door to open a crack and it can easily be pushed wide open. Your client's icon-giving friend is now offering a book about saints.

Damnable saints—all of them one-time clients who managed to become very pleasing to the Enemy. In most cases they are never canonized or long remembered, but some are placed on the church calendar—a kind of memory device—and held up as models. Not that they were in reality the flawless people they are generally made out to be. Far from it. Nonetheless, they evaded us in the end.

Sanctity is supposed to be something normal—something anyone can achieve. It's the Enemy's idea that each person, even the most ordinary, ought to be a saint, and even today it happens all too often.

More detail about the actual book given to your client would be useful. Have you the title and author? Are the saints

described all from a certain period? The early church? A
later period? Or is it a collection that spans all of Christian
history?

If the book is about the early church, that is, before
Constantine, then it will be almost entirely about martyrs.
There was hardly any other category of saint during the first
three centuries. Thus it may not be harmful reading as your
client isn't likely to see the connection between today's
world and a world in which Christians faced extreme
persecution. He imagines he is living in a society that is not
at odds with Christianity. Quite the opposite—he lives in a
Christian society! After all, there are a dozen churches
within a five-minute drive from his house. The president or
prime minister, far from being a Nero or Diocletian, makes
his church-going as visible as possible, attends prayer
breakfasts, and has the G-word often on his lips.

Another positive aspect of books about the early martyrs is
that the stories are short. In most cases only the scantiest
biographical information has survived. Often even the
martyr's age is not known, still less what the person did or
what he or she said. There is little information on family
background, personal characteristics, economic
circumstances, vocation, etc. Thus there is not much for
today's modern reader to connect with. In many cases, the
absence of historical facts has been filled by fanciful stories
about miracles so remarkable (beheaded people still
announcing the deceased person's belief and the like) that
the virgin birth and the resurrection seem minor events by
comparison. For the modern reader, such tales are so
unbelievable as to be embarrassing. With some small
encouragement from you, this may in turn make your client

wonder if there is anything truly historical about all these martyrs. Might the "memory" of them be nothing more than ecclesiastical propaganda?

It is not only in biographies of the early martyrs that one finds distorted portraits. They can also be found in books about saints from every age, even in cases where there is a great deal of biographical material to draw on. It is something of a tradition in hagiography to leave out all the saint's sins and shortcomings and focus only on his or her virtues and positive achievements. Often a lot of invented detail is inserted, material the writer imagines will edify the reader. It might be claimed that the saint as an infant refused to nurse on Fridays, the day on which Christians traditionally fast in memory of the crucifixion. Even where there are no instances of infantile piety or fanciful miracles stirred in, the wrinkle-free saint found in such books is so perfect that today's readers will feel like they are reading about another species, not the flawed sort of creatures they are themselves.

This has been one of our side's most ingenious strategies— to make people think that saints are somehow inhuman, or at any rate so far outside the range of ordinary humanity as to be irrelevant for an ordinary person. As long as our clients think of saints as perfect people from long ago, people who were born with halos, there's little danger that they will be inspired by their example.

If you are lucky—and most likely you are—this is the sort of book that has been given to your client. I won't say such reading is good for him, but it will probably do him no harm. Such a book might simply convince him that he is not a potential possessor of a halo.

But you may not be lucky. From time to time one finds books that present a more complex portrait of saints in which it's clear they were not genetically predisposed to holiness, that what was admirable about them was achieved only with great difficulty and involved many failures along the way. In the event your client begins to think of the saints as "real people," then it would be best for him to concentrate on their flaws and imperfections. They weren't so great after all, etc.

I cannot recall a saint who came empty-handed to confession, not even in old age. As it's a form of prayer, we cannot make out what is said, but I can tell you it's time consuming hanging around when saints confess. Chatter chatter chatter!

Yours warmly,

Wormwood

Wormwood Message 29

TO: Greasebeek

FROM: Wormwood

SUBJECT: Damnation

My dearest Greasebeek,

Not only was your last report the shortest and most evasive to date, but I have become aware that you dared to suggest to Izdrack that the setbacks you have been experiencing with your client may be due less to your own errors and neglect than to your "mistake" in taking advice from me. I quote: "Had I been better advised, things might have gone differently."

Yes, he showed me the vile e-mail you sent him with the heading *"Confidential."* Did you think he would not tell me what you had said? He was overjoyed at what you told him—another chance to deliver a blow at Wormwood.

This is how you thank your benefactors.

While Izdrack assured me that he knew my advice was always sound and that he didn't for a minute take your comment seriously, there was an obvious gleam in his eye and leer in his expression. He has long had it in for me—ever since a mishap I had involving Screwtape and myself a long while back. Izdrack has a memory like flypaper.

Let me tell you that your idea of spreading blame in my direction will not only fail—it will backfire too. Far from getting me instead of your miserable self on the hook, you will find yourself on a hook made even bigger by your upstart impudence.

Be warned.

Wormwood

Wormwood Message 30

TO: Greasebeek

FROM: Wormwood

SUBJECT: A close call

My dearest Greasebeek,

You have no idea how close a scrape you've had in the past twenty-four hours. Your last report blew some fuses. The one thing I was able to enjoy was seeing Izdrack in such a state. It was like a nuclear melt-down, a mini-Chernobyl. Most enjoyable!

I grant you that the news that prompted his fury—an avalanche of set-backs regarding your client—would get the vitriol flowing in any right-minded demon, still more in a supervisor.

Your client has not only continued visiting churches but he has found a particular church he wants to join—All Saints—and has asked to be baptized. Also to be batpized is his wife, not to mention the impending baby. Husband and wife have begun "taking instruction" and regard themselves as catechumens, a word that only months ago neither of them even knew existed and couldn't have pronounced. Meanwhile, you report that they are praying before meals, discussing the Bible, talking about saints, reciting prayers in front of an icon before going to bed, giving up meat on Fridays, and planning to put in some time volunteering at a local soup kitchen. You note that these activities and interests have taken such a hold on your client that he hasn't had time to stay involved with the victims group and that, in any event, he has decided that his parents "didn't actually do such a bad job."

Izdrack was livid. Your name was enshrined in curses.

At first I thought your situation hopeless. I could only agree with him that, despite countless opportunities, you have wasted each and every chance that came your way.

Izdrack was on the verge of assigning to your client another demon, your classmate Cinderhead. You were to face a hearing for gross malfeasance. He had all but signed the order. Had he done so and the hearing gone against you... But one doesn't want to speak about such things.

A lesser demon would have agreed that you deserved an extended tour of Hell's deeper zones, especially after daring to blame your mentor, but then it crossed my mind that I, as your mentor, might suffer a similar fate. Nothing would please Izdrack more.

It wasn't easy, but in the end I managed to convince Izdrack that only now, having gotten to know your client reasonably well, can you be expected to achieve positive results. And, after all, this is your very first case. It's one thing to have done well at the Academy and another to succeed in actual practice. A certain amount of patience is in order. So, you are safe for the time being.

And, after all, the new situation regarding your client is far from discouraging! Once baptized, he will regard himself as being home free, safe as a diamond in a bank vault. He will ride for months, even a year or two, on a tidal wave of convert zeal. Reader that he is, he'll soon fill a bookcase with all sorts of religious rubbish—theology, church history, volumes about the Bible, lives of the saints, writings of the Church Fathers—until he thinks he knows more about Christianity than anyone else in the solar system. He will be more often at church services than a monk of Mount Athos.

But all tidal waves finally subside. Once the wave's momentum is spent, you will have opportunities galore.

I can hardly wait.

Warmly yours,

Wormwood